EVERYTHING
TALKS TO ME

Grace Note

When I see God in everyone and everything,
true vision becomes mine.

When I hear God in every voice and murmur,
I tune in to the entire Universe.

When I feel God in my every emotion, the whole
world with all its inhabitants becomes precious
and revered.

When my love is so profound that I can give it
to the mightiest as well as to the lowliest, I,
within the Divine Plan, am perfecting myself.

Thus it is that the cosmos resounds and reverberates
in and through us. Lifting our sights, we stand
in awe. With a thunderous whisper we muster
our deep-felt thanks—our eternal gratitude.

Indeed we have let everything talk to us.

Now at last we can cry out with joy, "I Read You Loud
and Clear, God."

EVERYTHING TALKS TO ME

Grace Speare

ELEMENT

ROCKPORT, MASSACHUSETTS • SHAFTESBURY, DORSET

BRISBANE, QUEENSLAND

First Element edition, 1994

Copyright © 1979 by Grace Speare and Robert Byars
Preface to this edition © 1990 by Grace Speare
Revisions to text for this Element Books edition © 1994
by Grace Speare

Published in the U.S.A. in 1994 by
Element Inc.
42 Broadway, Rockport, MA 01966

Published in Great Britain in 1994 by
Element Books Limited
Shaftesbury, Dorset

Published in Australia in 1994 by
Element Books Limited for
Jacaranda Wiley Limited
33 Park Road, Milton, Brisbane, 4064

Text design and compositing by Paperwork, Ithaca, New York
Cover ilustration © Hartsdale Camera & Portraiture Studio
Cover design by Max Fairbrother

Published by arrangement with Quicksilver Books, Inc.
Originally published by Dell/Quicksilver Books, 1979;
Berkley Books, 1982; and Paragon House, 1990.

Printed in the United States of America by Edwards Brothers, Inc.

Library of Congress Cataloging in Publication data available.
British Library Cataloguing in Publication data available.

ISBN 1-85230-593-2
10 9 8 7 6 5 4 3 2 1

To my beloved daughters,

Luana and Adina,

and to all of

God's children everywhere . . .

ACKNOWLEDGEMENT

With love and special thanks to my dear friend, Bob Silverstein.

A unique man, whose indefatigable efforts never diminished.

Continually charging from a high point of awareness—his positive and creative mind make manifest his valuable contributions to this project.

To this beautiful soul, I remain indebted . . .

GRACE

CONTENTS

 # PREFACE

A NOTE TO THE READER

I am profoundly grateful for the supreme opportunity to once again address the reader of this book.

We come together in order to remind each other that we are born out of the Divine Spirit and not grown out of the soil like a bunch of potatoes. Our gift of life is the creation of the whole cosmos. The divinity of our existence gives us the means of developing our individuality through love and sympathy to all and everything we encounter.

Since the first publication of this book, I have received literally hundreds of letters from readers encouraged by its message. It has confirmed in them the power of self-exploration. The common thread of these letters contains a basic concern: Now that I am discovering who I am, I ask, *what* difference can I make in this world?

All the difference!

You, I, everybody, indeed each member of the human race matters a great deal in making our world a better place. This is such an important fact to remember, today more than ever before. You hear so much about what terrible shape our world is in. Crime and drug use seem to be run-

ning rampant; racism continues to rear its ugly head around
the globe; and man continues to wreak havoc with his environment. But a negative outlook that dwells on these concerns is part of the problem, not the solution. When we realize that the world is in crisis largely because we see it that
way, that our negative expectations are perpetuating the
misery, then we'll recognize that each individual, through a
personal change of attitude, can make a tremendous difference in this world. Indeed, that is our challenge, the ultimate contribution.

Each and every person is endowed with something so
special and unique that is not present in any other person.
To bring forth that special something inherent in us we must
first become free from ourselves: our attachments, our in-
grained patterns, our early conditioning. That opens the
gate to the 'know thyself' concept which prevents us from
being led astray by the currents and negativities of our time.
We then observe how we have begun to pay attention to the
voice of the indwelling individual soul, our very own.

The Eternal, the permanent, lives within the details of
our daily lives. We must learn to distinguish between what is
temporary and what is eternal. Thus, it isn't necessary to be
an enlightened master, a wealthy philanthropist, or a re-
nowned politician in order to make a difference. We simply
need to live our daily lives with a greater awareness of our
connection to everyone and everything we meet.

You are truly that special person who comes to make a
difference. Every individual human being makes a difference
here on earth. No one, absolutely nobody roams this world
insignificantly. No one, absolutely nobody is a mere speck
blotting the landscape of planet earth. We all count. We all
have that special something to contribute that no one else
can, in accordance with our own talent, ability, character,
that does not duplicate in any other person. But to find that
special spark of our own individuality we need to really learn

to know the human heart. And to know the human heart we must first look into our own being, our own soul, in seriousness and with a sense of honest self-exploration.

The whole mystery of our universe is one of the biggest questions asked of us. Paradoxically, we, everyone of us wandering about on this planet is actually an answer to this riddle. Deep within our own being lies the solution to the cosmic mystery. Knowing thyself is the foundation to knowing the world and our place in it.

We continue to learn as we journey through life. And what we learn from our experiences we then individualize in and through ourselves, which then makes all the difference in how we handle life and people in a more loving and caring way than we did the time before. For as long as our individual soul lives within our physicality we have the extraordinary opportunity to learn and to apply that which we have learned toward our own enlightenment.

We learn to love from our own experiences of hate—just as the pain and suffering we feel on our own skin or in our own heart teaches us to identify with the pain and suffering of others. The more traumatic the anguish we experience, the quicker we go through a sensitizing and purification of self and our own blood flow. In this way, we are never again insensitive to the plight and sorrow of others.

It cannot be stated enough: You make all the difference! You count for something so extraordinary when love and compassion rule your every mode of living. You are truly the most valuable person when kindness and tenderness are a generous part of your totality. Thereby you make your most creative contribution to life, to this planet and all its inhabitants. Bear in mind, your personal importance makes so vast a difference that without you there can be no planet earth.

CHAPTER ONE

EVERYTHING TALKS TO ME

Young men dream,
Old men have visions.
But women prophesy!

A DECK OF CARDS

Ever since I can remember I have been fascinated by dreams, faces, clouds, coffee grounds . . . anything. They all talk to me. Everything does. And everything could talk to you, too, if you would let it. It's only a matter of tuning in.

As a youngster, spending much time outdoors, my eyes were skybound. The skies intrigued me. In the formations of the clouds and their movements, I saw images that wove into storylike sequences. Sitting on the grass with a friend watching the clouds, I would describe vignettes which appeared to me like movies on a screen. Then days or even weeks later, the friend would run up to me and say, "Remember the things you told me about? The things you saw in the clouds? They happened, just as you said they would!"

At first I was surprised and thought, "Could there really be something to it?" But by and large I didn't pay it much mind. I was just talking, off the top of my head, not really hearing what I was saying. The words were simply coming through me somehow. My eyes remained fixed on the skies, day and night, and I found myself mesmerized, as though secrets were being revealed to me. To this day my eyes are skybound. The first thing I do upon awakening, and the last thing before retiring for the night, is search out the sky.

From an early age I was also intrigued with palmistry and dreams. I especially sought out books on dreams—although I could only find technical ones—and was endlessly asking people to tell me their dreams, so I could probe them and see if my interpretation fit that person. These were my pastimes as a child. I never had a toy in my life, and dolls just didn't interest me.

While I was still very young, I discovered dozens of games to play with an ordinary deck of cards. From games I went to a sort of fumbling and fooling around with the deck. I used to *feel* the cards in my hands, sensing a friction in them, as though they became a living thing that spoke directly to me. In playing with cards in this manner, I found myself making predictions. Perhaps to make myself feel important, I'd utter a few words with authority to other children to impress them. Little did I know that what I had said actually pertained to them, as I was to find out later. From that time on, wherever I went, I always had a deck of cards with me.

I wasn't yet fifteen when I went on a visit to Turkey. I had been invited by a young man, a friend of my family, who, was going home for summer vacation to Ankara, where his parents had a house. An elderly woman who lived next door, a professional card reader, came over to visit one day. We talked briefly and, as she left, she said to me, "Come to my house tomorrow. I'll read you." And I heard myself reply, "Okay. I'll read you, too."

I found her very perceptive, and when she had finished with the reading, I was quite impressed. I then proceeded to read her in my own fashion, and she remarked over and over again, "That's right. Yes, that's correct. You're very good at it." Whereas I had always simply felt the cards and fumbled with them, waiting for things to come through, she had a detailed and specific system, which was quite new to me. She had divided time into the past, present, and future. There were definite meanings and symbols represented by each card.

I immediately decided to adopt her system. It came naturally to me and took no study at all. Somehow I learned those symbols instantaneously. It was not a question of memorizing. Whatever she pointed out—the symbology, the patterns, the spreads of the cards, and the combinations—I just knew them instinctively. Anything you learn right away without studying comes because you have done it so often in other lifetimes; you merely trigger your memory. It was in this way that I picked up her basic technique of reading cards.

I use her system to this day and have since shared it with others. But I confess that in doing a reading I don't consciously know what I'm saying, and that still amazes me. Something simply takes over. The process is automatic. It's very much like walking downstairs; if you stop to think about what you are doing, you might trip and fall. As long as I am Grace, the conscious mind, nothing will come through. When Grace, the personality, is removed, however, something flows through me which is useful and constructive to others. But if I willfully say to myself, "Grace, get out of the way," the process doesn't work. l have to *allow* it to happen. I have to still my intellect and let the subconscious mind take over, without the ego interfering.

Not long ago I was invited to a swimming party with my daughters. One of the guests happened to be a theatrical agent who was very taken with my younger daughter, Adina. She knew of a part for a child in an upcoming Broadway play and felt certain that Adina would fit the role. A few days later we attended an audition. Adina was called back for further consideration. By this time my excitement began to mount. Out of more than 200 children who had tried out only three remained. Adina was one of them and it now seemed that she had a real chance to appear in a Broadway show.

The day after the second audition, as I was shuffling the cards for a reading, I found myself emotionally carried away. Adina. On stage. On Broadway. I was so excited that I was not able to proceed with the reading. Excusing myself, I got up from the table and went into my bedroom, where I meditated briefly to "empty" my mind. When I returned, Grace the personality was gone. In order to focus on the reading, I cannot let my ego get in the way of the material being transmitted. All channels must be free and open.

Until a few years ago I had only done readings as a lark, as a fun sort of thing at parties or someone's home. But then one day my husband walked out, and I was left in financial difficulty, facing mortgage payments and other bills.

Soon afterward the children's father announced he would no longer pay for my daughter Luana's piano lessons at the conservatory where she had been studying for a number of years. That did it for me. I reasoned with myself: all right, we don't have much food; we're threatened with foreclosure by the bank; and the bills are piling up. But the idea of Luana not continuing to express her talent stirred something deep within me. Her music lessons would be continued, that much I knew. I had to find work. At that point, I said, "I will do anything, even if it means scrubbing floors."

When I explained my decision to a close friend, she said, "Why look for a job? Why don't you do readings professionally?" It had never crossed my mind. I'd been doing readings for years and never thought of myself on that level. I told her I wouldn't know how to get started, but she said, "Leave it to me." She owned a clothing store and offered to tell her customers how good I was—word of mouth would do the rest. I wasn't too sure of myself but decided to give it a try.

My first client was a man. When the doorbell rang, I was more nervous than he. I was literally shaking. Doing a reading for money, albeit only $5, took on a totally new perspective. Afterward I was pleasantly relieved when be mentioned how valid the insights were and how accurately his problems had been pinpointed. When he left, I sat down to thank God for the fact that I had received direct guidance.

I needed $265 for Luana's next semester at the conservatory, so I vowed that every dollar I made from the readings would go exclusively toward that end. When I had gathered $255, at $5 per reading, the phone rang. It was the director of the conservatory. Auditions were to be held in two days for three available scholarships and he wanted Luana to try out for one.

We arrived, nervous and excited. The scene was bedlam. Hundreds of children from all over the New York area were milling about the conservatory grounds, waiting to audition. Hours later, they called Luana's name, and she and I jumped up. I kissed her and said, "I know you'll do well." She was a bundle of nerves. My ear was pressed to the door as she played for the judges. She emerged relieved, with a nervous little smile. I told her, "You were fantastic." Uncertain, she asked me, "Do you really think so?"

When the phone rang the next morning, I recognized the director's voice. "It gives me great pleasure to tell you that your daughter is a recipient of a scholarship," he said. Choking back tears, I mumbled my appreciation. I ran to meet her bus after school and cried, "Luana! Guess what!" She answered, "I know. I got the scholarship." When I nodded, she couldn't believe me. We hugged, we kissed, and we wept.

When I recovered from my excitement, I realized what this experience was saying to me. Obviously, the conservatory was not the real reason I was doing the readings. There was a more important purpose. God had shown me that readings were to be my life's work. Money was an incidental factor. It was a beginning that led to additional opportunities to reach wider audiences through talks to groups and occasional appearances on radio and television. To this day, however, the most important aspect of my work as a reader is on a one-to-one basis.

WE ARE ALL PSYCHIC

People don't realize how easy it is to predict. Everything is so predictable—especially people. Ouspensky writes about being in Russia with Gurdjieff, where they had formed a self-study group. Gurdjieff would take his followers on seemingly aimless walks through the woods. He always ran ahead of the group dropping various objects along their way such as papers, garbage, and trinkets. Then he would watch what each member in the group would do. There were those who felt compelled to pick up the object. There were others who would look and wonder, "Should I or shouldn't I?" Some members of the group might see the object and simply not be bothered by it. Still others didn't see anything at all!

Later Gurdjieff would confront the group with their reactions, proving to them that they could not go against their own individual character. The one who picked up the object was compelled to pick it up; he could not act in any other way. Out of his own neuroses, his unbreakable patterns of reaction, he *had* to pick it up. This principle applied equally to all the persons in the group. No matter what they did, they reacted automatically, in accordance with their own habitual patterns.

With such maneuvers, Gurdjieff demonstrated that everyone's personality was so steadfast that no matter what he does, he does so because be could not do otherwise. Gurdjieff played these kinds of games to shock people into a new awareness of themselves. Since most people sleepwalk through life, it is easy to make predictions about their behavior patterns.

By simply looking at a person's basic expression, you're ready to make a prediction. The other day I was in an elevator with another woman. In just the few moments we were together, something about her registered very clearly with me. I said to her, "You're a judge, aren't you?"

"How did you know?" she replied with amazement.

Everyone generates his or her own atmosphere, which is picked up by others, whether they're aware of it or not. For example, we may meet someone and say to ourselves, "Well, he'll never amount to much." Or, "She'll go far in life." When you see the person's gestures, when the person talks, when you hear his tone of voice, it gives you even further insight. And as people reveal themselves more and more, things become that much more predictable. You can glean so much, even from a fleeting exchange of impressions.

When we make predictions solely through the conscious mind, however, the room for error is immense and we must be very careful, because the conscious mind includes the ego and, therefore, judgment. People inevitably have a preconceived image of me, because their first contact is usually by phone. Although I was born in Germany, I went to school in England. They hear a British accent and immediately assume that because I'm a reader, I'm a fat old biddy. They've latched on to this popular image, and their own ego projects what I must be like. Every time I open the door to new clients, their eyes never meet mine. They look downward, as though expecting to see a midget. By the time they see me, I invariably hear, "Are you . . . Is Grace here?" Somehow they're surprised that I'm actually the opposite of what they imagined. Although she's come to me at least four times, one client to this day still says, "You don't look like a reader."

If you really care to look at someone, *without considering yourself*, your level of predictions will change dramatically. Try sitting quietly across from another person, stilling your mind and focusing your attention totally on her. A great deal will come through—without any kind of mediumship, cards, or voice.

We all make predictions. I merely do it on a deeper level,

because during a reading, my full attention is devoted to the subject.

What takes place in a reading? The extraction from the subject's subconscious mind of that which is already there, in order to bring it to his or her conscious attention. My subconscious mind contacts his subconscious mind. This enables him, based on his individual potential, to see his situation anew.

The subconscious mind is one mind, available to all. This is how it is possible for us to pick each other up psychically. And this is essentially how readings take place, no matter what medium is used: coffee grounds, tea leaves, palmistry, cards, séances, psychometry—whatever. The medium is merely a symbol, a key. A person may come to see me with a "show-me" attitude: "Let's see how great you are." If I allowed my ego to dictate, I would be irritated or have my feelings hurt. Instead, I simply shuffle the cards six times; on the seventh, the subject cuts the deck. During, this process, which I do automatically, I meditate and the personality across from me dissolves. Now I can tune in to her subconscious mind, bypassing whatever attitude she has brought in with her. A rapport is established which allows the creative, constructive process to come to the fore.

I've given several classes in card readings to people who want to become readers. I've found that most students don't enter into it with enough seriousness or depth, or else won't stay with it long enough; so, I discourage them. On the other hand, if a person is serious, sensitive, and intuitive, and if his desire is strong enough, I will teach him.

I taught one fellow who had remarkable sensitivity. I knew from the moment I laid eyes on him that he'd make an excellent reader. He's working in New York City now, and doing very well. He doesn't even have to have you present—in fact, he prefers that the subject not be around him. He'll speak to you by phone, and then proceeds to go through the spreads of the cards and the symbology. He then writes it all out and mails the reading to you!

Personally, I prefer to work face to face with the subject, because I feel that her presence, through vibrational currents, contacts my subconscious mind more directly. One of my former students still comes to me occasionally as a client. She knows all the symbology and is quite good at readings on her own, but she'll watch me reading her and sometimes ask, "Where did you get that from?" In all honesty I don't know. That's the part that cannot be taught. I've found it interesting, as I've taught, how loosely I actually work, and how I never restrict myself to the symbol. There are many things that enter in. When a particular card appears, I look at what it symbolizes. In another sense, I'm not really seeing it. There is a feeling, seeing, and hearing beyond the ordinary senses. The card is important, but it's not the thing itself. The symbol is valid and usually corresponds to the subconscious insight; but many times it works in reverse and the insight corresponds to the symbol, somewhat like a cross-reference.

What makes a good reader? What makes a good carpenter? Or a good musician? No matter what you do, you always want to do a better job. I always remind myself of this, because within the readings, there is constant growth and improvement. The more experienced we become, the more we perfect our given talents. There are always new insights to be gained through readings which can then be incorporated into the work. Channels open that were closed before, revealing newer and higher spiritual worlds.

More and more frequently I sense, smell, hear, or see a spirit present during a reading, often a close relative of the subject who died some years ago. Since the subject may be somewhat doubtful about such a presence, the spirit communicates to me the cause of its demise. The subject will often be quite taken aback by this information and subsequently will be better prepared to listen. Such disembodied souls are usually seeking forgiveness for love unexpressed when they were in this life. This forgiveness-seeking may be the real reason the subject is seated across from me.

Even at our best, we can do better. Readings can always improve. We can always see more, though we may never truly see everything. If a reading is not truly excellent, it is I who is at fault. I am always striving to come to more, to give more, to grow more in this work. The process of perfection is forever unfolding.

I'll never forget the first time I gave a class in readings. I mentioned it casually to a friend, and she panicked. "Are you crazy?" she said. "Don't give away your secrets! People will learn how, and then they won't need you anymore!"

But nothing is exclusively ours, and therefore no one can steal anything from us. The more I give, the more I shall receive. I can only learn by giving what I have to share, and from such giving, shall I receive tenfold. Everything that we give, we gain from.

IT DEPENDS ON THE INDIVIDUAL

Everything is known. We can have the answers to everything if only we go about it in the right way. There isn't a problem we encounter where we can't simultaneously glimpse its solution, because they're one and the same thing. The conscious mind begins to dwell on the problem, constantly rehashing it. By deliberately shifting our attention *away* from the problem, we make room for the solution to appear. If you attend a talk or a symposium, you will find people have great difficulty asking the right question because intuitively they know that *within their question lies the answer.*

As we attempt to change, as our beliefs and conceptions change, we experience all sorts of throwbacks from the past. Old problems and habits often intrude very sharply into our experience, which starts us *doubting* all over again. So we need reassurance to confirm something we already know in order to stay with it and grow. By giving in to the power of habit, the patterns we are accustomed to, we begin to waver. Then we need a jolt back into reality, the truth, to reaffirm that which we have already assimilated.

Many times during readings I get shudders or goose bumps, and sometimes a sensation of blood rushing to my head. The people I'm reading also go through similar reactions. I can often see their color change, because something is so true. Blushing or changing color are reactions people have no conscious control over; the response is involuntary and relates to the intuitive center in us. If something comes up that the subject knows to be true, his whole system will go through a bit of a shock. Even if he glimpses only a possibility, all the cells in his body are affected.

When a deep inner resource is touched, the self-consciousness of the person is involuntarily discarded. To some extent we are all self-conscious. What is self-consciousness? It's separating yourself from the world around you by building a wall that divides "you" from "it." But when a truth pierces our assumed, acquired defenses and reveals our true being, the ego suddenly loses control. The inner being comes to the forefront, and the ego part of us automatically falls away.

I read a young man recently—a beautiful soul—who had been under psychiatric treatment for a number of years. The experience had led him to believe that there was something wrong with him. He doubted his own spiritual tendencies, which were not dealt with in his therapy. He had never been to a reader before and had no idea what it would be like, but he told me afterward that the reading had confirmed many things for him that he had felt inwardly for a long time and had never expressed.

It is very helpful to come to someone who is on the positive side of life to reconfirm your own feelings. We all need this at times, and readings can help. I allow people to come back and be read again, because it serves to reinforce some-thing in them which might be vacillating. (Provided, of course, it's not done to excess. Anything that becomes a crutch is a detriment.) Even people who are seriously work-ing on themselves can come to a crossroads in life and begin to doubt. Although they know what the choice ought to be, they need to hear it again. They want to tune in to someone sharing the same wavelength to assure them that their newfound discoveries are correct. For that reason, I agree to see them again.

This is quite different from people who come and ask, "Weave us a beautiful story, a fairy tale." For the moment, they're transported into another reality, and then they go back to their lives as before—until they feel the need to be entertained again. These are the people I dissuade from re-turning to see me.

Anyone with so much influence must be very careful. People are always very amenable to suggestion, and this cre-ates an added responsibility. Many times when people are told something of the future they are immediately inclined to make it happen.

There's an Edgar Allen Poe story in which a man is told by a reader that he will commit a murder. He is deeply troubled by this prediction, and his life becomes more and more miserable as time passes while he awaits his violent act. Several years have gone by, the murder hasn't occurred, and he is a wreck. On a foggy night in the middle of a bridge he chances to run into the reader who gave him the predic-tion. Furious, he raves and rants, describing the torture he has been living through. His anger so carries him away that (you guessed it) he kills the reader!

In a reading there are so many things that hinge on, are dependent on, the individual. A prophecy is not a rigid thing. It falls into the realm of possibilities, and therefore deals with individual potential. When they receive any kind of prophecy, most people try to fit themselves into it and make it happen, and that certainly is not the purpose of a reading. (In a sense, things are predestined; in another sense, they're not.)

There's an old tale concerning two priests arguing about predictions. It dates back to the Babylonians, to a time when people lived their lives by prophecy, when nothing of importance was done without consulting a seer of some sort. One priest says to the other, "You cannot avoid your destiny." The other replies, "You make your own destiny." The first priest gives an example of a man who was told he would die by something falling on his head. To escape his fate, he moves to the desert, where there is no possibility of anything falling on him. But one day a bird carrying its prey drops it, striking the man on the head and killing him instantly. The second priest tells a story of a man who was preparing to take a caravan across the mountains to a distant city. An oracle he consults foresees him being trampled by horses. The man then changes his plans and resolves not to go on the trip. Later he learns that others who made the journey met the tragic fate predicted. The first story deals with predestination, the second with free will.

But the truth lies in neither one story nor the other. Nothing is so totally predestined that cannot be altered by a conscious act of will—a will that links with God. The man in the first story accepted the concept of death, and through his fear attracted it even in the desert. The man in the second story chose to live and death ignored him. There are many different roads we can choose to travel. That's where free will enters in. Our own choices play a tremendously important part in how we arrive at our destiny.

I remember a woman, a regular visitor of mine, who projected a great amount of negativity. The cards indicated that her husband was shortening his life through self-indulgence and self-rejection and that, unless drastic changes occurred in his daily life, she would soon lose him. One day she sent her husband to me. In his reading, a program was indicated:

He was to follow a specific diet. Lots of salt-free, sugar-free high-protein foods, plenty of water to cleanse his system, yellow vegetables, certain fruits, and above all, a positive attitude toward life. Ofttimes, particular things come up. No two readings are alike, just as no two individuals are alike. There is something unique to every person which is not duplicated in any other reading.

A few weeks later, he wrote me. In ecstatic terms he described how he had begun following the indicated projections right away, and that the tests he underwent showed immediate improvement. By the second week all his test results were normal. He called me often to share with me the many changes that were occurring for him, how he had begun to look forward to things and make plans for the future. He had changed from a dying man into a happy, vibrant individual. So, too, had his wife. Abandoning himself completely and totally to this program, and setting to work with newfound faith, had produced positive change in this man's life.

What I would like to emphasize is the importance of the *faith* that any person should put into a new plan, a new thought. Total confidence and belief in a program, rather than the specific program itself, will urge your actions and become the catalyst for improvement.

Many people are helped by readings. It is particularly gratifying and brings my activity down to earth when I learn a reading I gave has been of direct help to another soul. We are all here in service to one another.

If I feel encouraged about my work, it's due mostly to those people who come in as if life is over, having no direction at all, and who leave with a new outlook. That's all it is, really: A different way of looking at a problem they've gotten stuck on. They may come in with shoulders hunched, head hanging low, resigned, depressed, and defeated. When the reading is over, they often stride out with their shoulders back, heads up, eyes looking bright and straight ahead toward their future. There are so many changes that can take place.

These changes may be temporary. Perhaps out on the street five minutes later they are back to their old thinking and behavior patterns. But the majority of people are affected by the experience in a more lasting way and will retain their uplifted feelings.

When my day is over, I don't consciously remember the readings because, as I've said, my subconscious mind has been at work. The subconscious mind registers everything—the minutest detail can be remembered and recalled. But the conscious mind cannot contain all this information and continue to function. The capacity of subconscious mind is infinite, a storehouse of everything we've ever experienced, accessible to us at any time. If need be, this is how I can recall a particular reading no matter when it occurred. A subject may call to tell me details from her reading. As she reviews it, my subconscious memory is triggered. I may not remember who the person is or what she looks like, but subconsciously all material is indelibly recorded and can therefore be played back.

The caller usually goes on to tell me what she's done with the material which was projected, and what results she has gained. Mostly, she reports that she no longer dwells in the halls of the past, in negativities and in all the nonsense that she was into initially.

All of us—myself included—get stuck sometimes. We get stuck emotionally. But we are all dynamic and often need an outer stimulus to push us past that point, to guide us, and to get us back in motion again in the right direction.

Two Signs of Warning

After my husband left, debts began to mount, and I eventually decided that I would have to sell the house. But aside from the obvious things, the debts and all, what convinced me to do it, what really talked to me, were two things.

On the side of the house where my bedroom was birds came to harass me. No matter what I did, no matter what gadgets or tricks I used, I couldn't get rid of them. I had heard birds were afraid of snakes; so I took a few of Adina's toy snakes and placed them on a windowsill where they were plainly visible. But the birds weren't frightened; instead, I was frightened. Forgetting I had put them there, I would walk into the room and scream.

Of course, they were making an incredible mess all over the outside wall of the house. Then I remembered how, in the Bible, Joseph had interpreted the dream of his fellow prisoner. The man had dreamt that he had three baskets on his head and that birds were picking at one of them. Joseph interpreted this as a dream of death. So, I reminded myself, "Indeed, when do birds come and crap all over you? When you're dead!" They are like vultures, who come to prey on you. I realized that these birds were seeing me dead. This was the first sign that I should leave the house. However, instead of doing something decisive, I had the house painted, figuring the smell of the paint would drive the birds away. It did—for about two days. Then they were back again, fouling the wall as usual. I was outside daily, hosing it down.

I tried to surprise the birds, to frighten and disorient them. I would move the sliding windows of my bedroom abruptly to make a noise which would startle them away, but they would come right back. After a while, we were playing a game: They'd be flying near the house, I would throw open the bedroom window, they'd fly away, I'd go back to what I was doing, they'd return. Back and forth. Whenever I had a spare moment, I would throw open the window, which eventually broke. And they were still around. I finally realized that these birds were conveying a very strong message to me: "It's time to get out, Grace."

Then came the second, the most important thing that talked to me. One morning, about a month before I actually sold the house, I woke up and looked out the window. I had a view of a stone wall and a golf course beyond that. But as I looked out that morning, I saw a cross and a cemetery instead. I was sure I was hallucinating. "This can't be," I reasoned to myself. "I've lived here for twelve years and have never seen such a sight."

I went down to the living room and looked again. I still saw the same thing. Every day after that I would look out, doubting my sanity, and see that morbid sight. Finally I asked Luana to take a look in that direction and tell me what she saw. With a puzzled voice she said, "That's funny. I see something I've never seen before. I see a cross, and it looks like death."

To me this was the strongest, clearest message I had received: "You're dying where you are. You have overstayed your welcome. Get out!" When I had advertised the house for sale weeks before, I was still vacillating. "Where will I go? Is it the right thing to do?" I hadn't given up my attachment to the house. However, when I realized the meaning behind these two obvious messages, I decided I must move.

Once having made the decision, I knew in my mind the house was sold. As long as that house was rightfully mine, there were no disruptions. Once I knew that I was getting out of that house, then I was certain the buyers would appear. The next day, when they did, I knew the sale would be harmonious, without bickering. From the first moment the couple walked in, it was obvious they were the buyers. It was just right for them. Having loved the house so, I couldn't have sold my home to just anybody. It had to be beneficial for all concerned: a happy thing for them and a right thing for me.

It bothered me that I had never told them about the birds. I felt a little guilty about it, because I had kept the wall hosed down so they wouldn't spot the evidence. A few weeks after they had moved in, we went back to visit and pick up the mail. I humorously asked the wife if she had gotten to know that wonderful family of birds that used to come to the bedroom windows.

"What birds?" she asked. "We haven't noticed any birds." Later, I walked outside to check the wall, and to my amazement it was perfectly clean. How much more specific can something be? How much more clearly can you see that things are talking directly to you? The message obviously had been for me, not for the people who bought the house.

SOME INCIDENTS AT PARTIES

Several times I have been called on to be the entertainment at a party. Some people hire a band and some people want a reader. One time, since there were so many people present that night, I read the married couples together to save time.

One couple came in to be read. The wife was very pretty, but totally lost; the ground had vanished from under her. The husband was lost, too, but in his own loud way he put on a front of self-confidence. He was a rowdy, materialistic person. The reading clearly indicated that their son needed help; and the marriage also needed help. I came right to the point about it.

The husband immediately flared up. "I didn't want to come here! I don't believe in all this junk!" His wife was touched, however, and admitted that they did have a big problem with their boy.

"It's out of your hands, because you're not handling it properly. He needs professional help," I told them.

The wife replied, "He's on hashish, and he's beyond help."

With that, the husband jumped up and shouted, first at me and then at his wife. I shall spare you his language. He had noticed the various ways I had counted and laid out the cards. I was using the club suit for their reading. His assumption was that my discards—the red suit, which did not apply at all to either one of them—represented his wife and that I was favoring her. He was certain that I was reading him through the black cards, and to him black stood for everything that was bad. In his anger he believed that I was "cheating" in some way to slant things against him. Then his wife started cursing him. They were really going at it. When I told them that the session was at an end, the woman desperately pleaded, "Tell me how many broads he's been seeing!"

It was a devastating scene, and I got such a clear picture of a lost soul, their son, totally oblivious to life as a result of drugs. Through their own words, their violent feelings, I could see how they would come to destroy their very lives. It could not go any other way, unless they turned their lives around.

Later, an attractive young woman came in alone, and I asked, "Where is your husband?" Although the single people were to come in alone, somehow I knew she was married. She simply said, "He didn't want to come in."

Almost as soon as the reading began, she was reaching into her purse for tissues to dry her tears. I said, "You're paying a very heavy price for the money you've gotten. I'm talking about big money. But for this big money you have sold your soul, and you cannot live with it any longer. You're going to run away." Nevertheless, I was able to see another marriage in her life; one based on love instead of money.

Afterward, she talked to a friend of mine. "I can't believe it," she said. "How can she know all this?" This pretty girl in her twenties had married a seventy-five-year-old multimillionaire on the rebound of a broken-up love affair. She had decided she wanted money, and she had gotten it. Moreover, she told my friend that she had indeed begun planning to leave this man.

Later, when I heard all of this, I thought, "How little we think of ourselves." And how cheaply we sell ourselves, only to find that it makes us miserable. We simply can't compromise ourselves to that extent without paying another, much higher price.

I once was reading a couple at another party, and I told the man, "You are facing a wonderful opportunity which you don't want to take. It is a position in public life, but it cuts your monetary intake in half. Unless you do it, however, you will never find yourself."

"This is incredible," he remarked. "I was just approached for public office, and I'm considering it. Of course, it pays nothing; but it's a chance to do something really worthwhile." He said he really couldn't decide what to do, but that he was inclined to stay with making money. Later, as often happens, he said to me, "Gloria [the hostess] must have told you about me." And I said, "Certainly. Every word."

Another time, I was asked to read the guests at a dinner party given by a prominent newscaster for one of the major networks. His wife had attended one of my talks and contacted me. I hardly remembered her when I arrived, and I didn't know anyone else there at all.

There were fourteen guests, so it wasn't possible to give each of them a life reading. I used a shortened version instead, employing one spread of the cards, which I sometimes use if people have a specific question. We had agreed that I would allow ten minutes for each person.

There were two psychiatrists among them, and the reaction of one of them was priceless: He swore that the hostess had told me everything. "Otherwise, how could you know?" he said. "There is no other way for you to know these things. I am sure of this, because I certainly know the human mind." This was the reaction of most of the men there that night. They were all professionals and were very secure in their skepticism.

In one man's reading, it was projected that he helped people with their heart ailments, but that he had neglected his own; and that he should go and see a doctor, even though he was a heart specialist, for his heart was ailing. He was very touched by this, because he had known it all along, but would not admit it—even to himself. This kind of thing is true for all of us, whatever we are engaged in, whoever we are. If you see an actor specializing in playing heavies, or characters that die or commit suicide, chances are the pattern will reproduce itself in his life. And the entertainer who endlessly sings those unhappy love songs will likely die of a broken heart. Likewise, doctors seem to attract their very specialties—cancer, heart disease, whatever.

The men at this party were convinced that the readings were all a hoax; except for the heart specialist, who, before they all left, let me know how helpful the reading had been. Some of the women thought it was exciting, but even they were sure the hostess must have given me some information. Certain people are unwilling to admit the possibility of anything outside of their reason and training, and with them you simply can't win. If you're right, someone must have told you. If a certain detail is wrong, you know nothing and it's all nonsense. Either way, they are safe.

A few days later, the hostess called me and among other things told me the majority of her guests were totally convinced that she had filled me in on all the details of their lives. She knew very well that she hadn't—and that had set her to thinking. Now she wanted a reading for herself, but she didn't want anyone to know about it!

TIME DOES NOT EXIST

About ten years ago, I went to see a woman who was a reader. She lived in New York City, and I had heard good things about her. But whatever she told me seemed like utter nonsense to me at the time. She said things about a marriage which were so farfetched that I didn't pay any attention. Then she said, "You're a writer," and went on to talk about a book I was going to write. That made no sense to me, either. Later, if people asked me what I thought of her as a reader, I said, "She's terrible!" (just as some people may talk about me, I'm sure). Nothing she told me at that time seemed applicable at all. As it turned out, most of what she told me has come to pass, but I simply could not connect with it then.

Today people come to me always wanting to know who, what, where, how, and—most of all—when. But a reading just isn't that specific, because on the subconscious level there is no time. This is difficult for people to accept, since they are usually consumed with time and other details. Moreover, it's quite possible to literally kill a prophecy with this kind of obsessive concern with time.

I'll never forget one woman, who actually was one of the first people I read professionally. Three months after her reading I was in a restaurant and she appeared out of no-where and began to attack me verbally. "You don't remember me, do you?" she said. "I came to you several months ago, and you told me that a man was waiting around the corner for me. And I have looked around the corner, and there hasn't been any man!"

She was creating quite a scene, and all I could do to sub-due her was to tell her that I truly didn't know what she was talking about, but if she was unhappy about the reading, and it would make her feel any better, she could come back for another reading, and I would not charge her for it.

Six months went by, and I received a phone call. There was a shrieking voice on the line, attacking me, and I recognized it. I simply repeated my offer.

Three months later (it had now been a year since the original reading), she showed up to try again. But no matter what came through in the reading, she would immediately start shouting at me. "You told me the same garbage a year ago!" Finally, I apologized and said I could only read whatever was projected, and that I felt either a reading was not for her or she should seek out another reader. She insisted on paying anyway and angrily left.

Another six months had passed when she called me for the last time—but in a new tone of voice. "I owe you an apology," she began, and went on to describe how everything I had predicted was now taking place. She was preparing to marry a man who had indeed been around the corner, and the description of him had been completely accurate. The reading had also said that they would be uprooted, and they were now packing to move to Florida. She apologized again and said she wanted to get a gift for me to express her thanks. I almost couldn't help myself. I felt like telling her the best gift she could give me was to tell me she was getting married and was moving!

My subjects always want the times and the dates and the places, and a reading is not reduced to those kinds of details. I get a lot of complaints. "You told me this-or-that, and I'm still waiting!"

"Be patient," I tell them. I wish I could sit down with each person who comes to me and explain that time does not exist, that it is a figment of the intellect. So many people reduce themselves to time machines.

On the other hand, there are a lot of people who are truly open and searching, looking for guidance, who are at a crucial point in their lives, and who are looking for a way to move forward, wondering what is the right thing to do. For them a reading is very helpful. After that, it depends on how well they can sustain their enthusiasm. Doubts creep into everyone's mind. If things do not materialize immediately, the questioning starts. This doubt, this mistrust sets up its own energy, which attracts similar negative energy—and then people want to know why such-and-such hasn't happened. They don't realize they have a heavy hand in it. A happening will be; it is not restricted to time. Depending on the type of thinking and feeling going on within you, you can demonstrate a happening instantaneously.

This leads us to a much larger concept: faith, self, the integral part we play in the larger scheme of things, and the individual's relationship to all universal laws and to God. We need to enlarge our perspectives on life. *Life is eternal*, without specific beginning or ending—as opposed to the finite mind that wants to compartmentalize everything to make it all manageable and forgettable. You can't live within these limitations and progress. You have to constantly enlarge and see life anew—review it anew—in order to reach the Infinite mind.

TUNING IN

Everything talks to me; and everything could talk to you, too—if you would only let it. It's simply a matter of tuning in. All we are, really, are receivers, apparatuses that can tune in and refine ourselves to a higher frequency and even a higher dimension. We can tune in, but we have to prepare ourselves. At the same time, we are transmitters, because we cannot receive unless we transmit. Your input is your output.

The more refined our instrument becomes, the better we can transmit or receive. The more we give love, the more love we shall receive. The more we give of anything, the more we shall get back. Everything is there for us to use; but we can only utilize it if we are in the act of giving it, of being it. The flow is continually returning to the giver, whatever we give. And for those who hang on, who cannot give, eventually that flow is cut off, and they cannot be given anything.

We have so much to give! In the act of giving we learn the process of life. We learn the value, the love of life. Life is so magnificent that the more we conceive of it, the more we will want to live; therefore, the longer we will live, because there are always "new" discoveries to make. The most important part of using what we know is sharing it with whoever touches our world.

🌺 CHAPTER TWO 🌺

THE SEA OF NEGATIVITY

*Never underestimate the power
of mass-thinking.*

MASS-THINKING AND MASS-HYPNOSIS

We are brought up in a sea of negativity. We are surrounded
by pessimism, immersed in guilt, and constantly torpedoed
by judgments—of others and especially our own. Giving up
this mass-thinking, this mass-hypnosis of despondency, is
the price we must pay in order to lead a creative, loving life.

Consider health, for example. It is commonly believed
that in the course of a year, or at a certain time of the year,
you must have a cold or two. Mass-thinking is very powerful: By drumming this expectation into the subconscious
mind, the colds are delivered.

Cause and effect. The important thing is what you believe. If you don't believe you're going to get a cold, you'll
never have one! A healthy mind maintains a healthy body.
The body can't think or act by itself; it's dependent on our
daily thinking, feelings, and actions. These generate our atmosphere, our overall mood, and general attitude. Happy
people are healthier people.

There are all kinds of mass-produced maxims we accept
blindly: you're too young to do this, you're too old to do
that, a woman can't be this, a man can't be that, and certain

things are dangerous. There are a thousand adages that are firmly embedded in our upbringing. But they can affect you *only when you let them*. Only when you consent do you give them power. You always have the choice to ignore them.

Recently I heard about a woman who gave birth for the first time in her life at fifty-seven. Her pregnancy had been approached with some concern; but the delivery took only twenty minutes and there were no problems. To me this was an inspirational news item, something truly out of the ordinary. Clearly she was rejecting mass-thinking, which says you have no business having a child after age thirty because you'll either drop dead or the child may suffer abnormalities.

We have no idea how much seeps through us, no matter how alert we are. We're continually being hypnotized from every direction: radio, television, songs, newspapers, and movies. We're almost always under hypnosis of one sort or another, whether it be subtle or very obvious.

What should be emphasized is also a form of hypnotism: We want to hypnotize ourselves into a right way of living. Just as we are hypnotized into the negative aspects of life, we can also suggest to ourselves the creative process of life. We can declare truth from the conscious mind into the subconscious mind. We're certainly capable of it, and the results are always wonderfully exciting. If you hypnotize your subconscious mind in the right way, it will correspondingly deliver the right experience to you. If you impress it otherwise, the experience shall be otherwise. Results are always evident, because life responds by correspondence.

In other words, you want to become very repetitious to yourself about all the beautiful affirmative things in life and your relationship to them. You want to hypnotize yourself so strongly that you can experience all the positive actions of life. If you observe negative persons, you will see that they are also under a form of hypnosis; they have practiced negatively and conditioned themselves, establishing a negative format that automatically produces all the wrongs in their lives.

You can hypnotize yourself one way or the other. What is an automatic action, except a form of hypnotism? Since this is a natural process, you certainly want to hypnotize yourself positively in order to experience life more constructively. The more you understand that what the conscious mind hammers and impresses into the subconscious mind becomes the actual action of your life later on, the more you will want to impress the subconscious mind into delivering affirmative experiences to you.

We don't have any idea how much influence television has on people's minds, how it slowly permeates our thinking. For instance, I have been using the same brand of toothpaste for years and I like it very much. But there's a new brand being advertised day and night, although I deliberately "tune out" whenever any commercial comes on. One day I went to the store and I didn't even look for my usual brand; I bought the new one. They got to me! Unconsciously! It's the hypnotic repetition, the constant hammering it home. Even if you think you're not listening, it's working on you.

It so happens I love the new toothpaste. So you could also say I was led to it, that I'm supposed to be using it. You can look at it from many different angles—if you allow everything to talk to you, as everyone should. Many times we make a move in a given direction, subconsciously, and it is a right move, a sort of guidance. Of course, toothpaste may seem an unimportant example; but still, subliminally we are always being led.

Mass-thinking also goes in cycles, but on a very selective basis. Right now we're in an era when many marriages seem to go asunder in our society and divorces are very popular. Marriage is a sacred union between two people. The selection of one another is really basically instinctive: Two souls coming together through some inner need born long ago from previous incarnations. If seen in this light, two people are able to work with each other on an entirely different plane and with an entirely different, attitude. A genuine sense of responsibility will then be assumed by each toward the other. Even though the personality is seemingly the attraction, matrimony between two people is the selection of the soul—and naturally this involves the law of karma.

The commercialism of our culture today advocates all the wrong things. The outer, materialistic world dictates everything. Divorce is currently in style. If you're not divorced once or twice, something must be wrong with you. Values are so misplaced that we are impressing the children—the adults of tomorrow—with the wrong kind of thinking. They've come to look on marriage as old-fashioned or else something you can go in and out of like a revolving door. All of this thinking relieves us of our own responsibility; we assume we have nothing to do with it.

In this way we retard the soul. With their sophisticated attitudes people have become very glib about such things as values. We talk about being free. Free from what? Imagine the impressions being sent out, on television for example, to a young receptive mind that doesn't know yet where it is going. Many children of today are modeling themselves unconsciously on negative stereotypes. Mass-thinking is dangerous and terribly irresponsible.

Negative Influences

Before her period, a woman is reputed to go into a depression. She doesn't have to, but most women have allowed themselves to succumb to mass-thinking on this. It's an excuse to feel negative, because society believes when you get your period certain things take over and you are allowed to feel depressed and self-pitying.

Recently, a neighbor complained to me of a miserable day she was having, which she quickly excused under the guise of this popular notion. She had a migraine and was really going at her children, yelling all sorts of things. As it was happening, she never sensed the damage she was causing to the fibers of her body, not to mention her kids. Often when we are on a kick like this, we feel falsely alive through our anger. Our energies are enormous for a while. We enjoy the negativity we are putting out.

We need to remind ourselves that we're not subject to such negative influences. Once we come to a larger understanding, we see how much bigger and freer we really are. We simply know better! When we do not handle our situation immediately, it takes days or even longer to undo the damage inflicted.

We can always be far greater than we are, but we need to put forth greater effort. We can't afford to let ourselves fall prey to mass-produced thinking, because when we do, we must suffer the consequences. When we are under mass-hypnosis, we come under its laws and are subject to its whims. In accepting the dicta of others, we merely provide ourselves with noble excuses.

We can't afford to slouch. We must always reach a little higher, and that demands diligence rather than acquiescence. We can always stretch our minds. We can always achieve more. The courage to be our own person demands our rejection of mass-produced thought. We must seek our own counsel in order not to pay a heavy price later for the negativity of today.

A FOOT, A TOOTH, AND AN ANKLE

When Luana was about six, she was fooling around with a large television set, and it fell down on her foot. I heard her scream and rushed to her room. I was through with intellectualizing and had begun demonstrating my beliefs. When I came in and saw what had happened, I said, "It's the best thing that could happen to you. It's wonderful!"

"But it hurts!" she cried. "Get a doctor!" Her foot was swelling like it was on yeast.

Denying that immediate reality, I assumed the next moment's reality, by seeing, feeling, and visualizing her foot in its perfectly normal condition. I mentally envisioned her walking normally, bouncing around. I said, "Get up and walk! And know that you are well. There's nothing the matter with you! I see nothing wrong with your foot. It is beautiful, it is whole, it is strong. Get up and walk!" For one so young she made a monumental effort. She got up and tried to walk, stumbled to the floor, and swore that she couldn't. And I, with a firm, strong voice, urged, "But you can!"

Anyone watching this scene would have thought, "What a cruel mother! She has no compassion, no feeling." I had my daughter walking back and forth across the room, over and over, tears streaming down her face, reminding her that she was in perfect health. I worked with her that way for an hour, during which time the swelling went away. We watched it disappear together. Suddenly she said, "I'm well! It's all gone." I'm not saying she didn't experience pain. But a truth was declared—and it materialized.

In terms of conventional medicine, an hour in healing is practically a miracle. Now, why did it work so fast with Luana? *Because she was only six years young and had not yet assimilated that much negativity into her life!* Were she older, she would have absorbed more mass-produced negativity into her subconscious mind, and in turn, her subconscious mind would have taken that much longer to effect a cure. By the time Luana was six, she had already been introduced to a lot of new thinking. When I came into her room, there was no doubt in my mind that she was healthy and her foot whole. I was steadfast; I had one hundred percent belief. I declared, "I know it's nothing, it's gone, it's disappearing into the nothingness it came from." And her subconscious acceptance took place within an hour.

As I looked at her foot, and it was enormous, in my mind's eye I actually *saw* it as normal. In declaring the truth into the ether, and knowing that everything we declare to the higher intelligence will be honored (the good or the bad), I saw the swelling diminish and the foot return to normal size. Then as I watched, it literally began to do that. Because of the imaginative faculty that we all have, whereby we can see the ought-to-be state, we can create our next moment of reality into visibility. In other words, what we see in our mind's eye, we can produce as a fact in our lives.

Before she was two, my younger daughter, Adina, fell down and dislodged one of her front teeth. It hung loosely from her gum. We had guests that evening, and immediately they all became hysterical doctors. I asked them to let me handle it myself. I took Adina up to her room and again declared a truth.

As she was bleeding and crying, I explained, "You see how this tooth is out of place? You wait and see; that tooth wants to get back to its home, but we have to give it a chance. You go to sleep, and when you wake up you'll see the tooth will have traveled back to its proper place."

She dried her eyes and said, "I know it," and went to sleep. She accepted her next moment's reality. While she was sleeping, I declared the tooth back to where it belonged— and I *saw* it there. That's all-important. You must deny that which you are seeing, that which stares you in the face, and instead *see* the actual state of becoming, thereby creating your next condition.

Early the next morning I was in her room when she awoke. The tooth had been utmost in her subconscious mind all night long and she immediately felt it upon awakening. The subconscious mind had come through, as it always does, and delivered the tooth to its rightful place. There was never a more excited child. "Mommy, Mommy, look! My tooth got back home!"

A similar incident happened to me several years later. I have two older brothers, and the eldest and I have been challenging each other since my birth. One afternoon when I was at the top of a flight of stairs and he was at the bottom, an argument started. Half angry, half joking, I picked up a pillow and threw it at him, whereupon I lost my balance and came tumbling down the stairs. I landed on a slate floor and cried, "My ankle! I can't move!" My brother helped me to my bed. He wanted to send for a doctor right away, but I refused. Although I was in excruciating pain, I wanted to be left alone.

My ankle grew to an enormous size. I was in terrible pain, but I was enjoying it because I was the center of attraction. Luana brought me my meals, and soon I had friends and neighbors stopping by to help out. I thought it was great. Of course, I wouldn't have a doctor. With what I knew, I didn't need a doctor. But I also didn't do anything for myself. I was simply lying there, watching TV (the Idiot Box, I call it), doing absolutely nothing. So, of course, the swelling never went down.

By about the third day, I said to myself, "What's going to be with you, Grace? How long are you going to nourish this garbage? Now get up, get out of bed, and start standing on your own two feet!" So I got up. As I put my foot down I noticed I did it with great care (the pain, you know). "Come on! Remember what you told Luana. Put your foot down and walk!" So I did, and soon the swelling had disappeared completely.

Here again, it was a projection of the inner eye, seeing myself whole and healthy. This is the process. I remember standing on that ankle and seeing stars—it was so agonizing. I said to myself, "How would I feel if that ankle were normal? I'd be floating on air." Then I assumed that feeling, and with my inner eye I saw my ankle in its normal state. Suddenly all that swelling began to vanish.

With Adina, being two years old, it worked within minutes. With Luana, at six, it took an hour. With me (never mind my age), it took three days. When we pay less attention to the negativity crowding our lives, we become more aware of the wonderful capabilities we are born with.

EDUCATION IS A MISNOMER

We know everything. Everything we know is already within our subconscious being, waiting to be sensed, contacted, and tapped. There is really nothing unfamiliar to us, nothing that is new. Only in our discovery, or rather rediscovery of our subconscious memory, do we find ourselves anew.

Therefore, all we need do is pull out from within ourselves the knowledge that is already inherent in each of us. Anything we supposedly learn in this life is merely refreshing our memory of experience we have dealt with before. This should be the approach of a teacher to a child: to assume that the child *already knows*, and to work from the point of view of "How can I refresh this child's memory?"

The teacher has as much to learn from the children as the children have from the teacher. The moment the teacher stops learning from the pupils, the true educational process stops. Children are naturally all subconscious memory and imagination; they express themselves freely. This is readily apparent if you truly focus on a child and observe him or her carefully. The problem in our society is that we do not pay sufficient attention to others, because we are consumed with ourselves. This is the barrier between teacher and child, or between parent and child; it prevents them from truly dealing with a child's individuality.

One day last winter Adina was in school and her teacher was talking about snowflakes, saying that every one has six sides. Adina disagreed with her teacher, believing that no two snowflakes are alike. Only two days earlier, Adina and I had been watching a magnificent snowfall. We talked about how fantastic it was that no two snowflakes are the same, and how rich nature is, never duplicating itself. Her teacher got very upset and told Adina to be quiet, continuing to talk about how they all have six sides, making all snowflakes alike. Finally, Adina interrupted her. "The next time we have a snowfall," she said, "look and see for yourself that no two snowflakes are alike." The teacher was furious because Adina wasn't accepting her dogma. That's how children are taught: "I am the teacher and I know, and you are the student and you are supposed to learn what I want to teach you!" Children are left so little room for their actual imagination and given no allowance for creative thinking or for true understanding. Rare is the teacher who inspires and motivates the child.

A teacher came for a reading recently. She was a compulsive talker, and anything I started to say she interrupted immediately with a contrary statement. I was shocked to learn that she was looking for a job at my daughter's school. This woman had all the qualifications—the right diplomas, the right credentials—but where was the person? Emotionally, she was unbalanced and irrational; nevertheless, she was qualified to teach because she had diplomas which entitled her to a position where, unfortunately, she would impose her neuroses on open, susceptible, amenable children. Imagine the influence this woman would have on a young mind.

Our system of education needs to be examined. The teacher I spoke of was just one individual, but if you take it on a larger scale, you'll find that in most schools the overall influence is extremely damaging. Too much emphasis is put on the intellect, data, information, statistics, and not enough on our inner beings. It is in sensing our *being* that we connect to the larger scheme of things. In our schools this aspect is not only neglected, but squashed with negativity. By ignoring the beingness of each child, we are mass-producing automatons. Teachers should know every individual child in the classroom intimately, no matter how large the class is.

When I was a little girl, I had to walk a long distance to

school by myself. From time to time I wouldn't go to school at all; instead, I'd go to a nearby park where I had selected a tree for myself in a quiet spot with no people about. There I'd spend the entire day sitting under my tree reading books—but not schoolbooks. The books I read were ones I had selected for myself in my thirst for learning and identification. I would do this for days on end, until the school eventually called my parents to ask where I was. Of course, my parents had no idea what was going on, so they asked me where I had been. I told them I had been in school, and that there must have been some mistake. I would go back to school for a few days, and then I would start skipping classes again.

One day my father decided to follow me. He tells the following story to this day. I had gotten to my favorite tree and was busy reading when he came up behind me and asked, "What are you doing here?" I just looked up at him blankly as if he were a total stranger. He asked me again, but couldn't get a reply out of me. He yanked me by the arm and led me off to school, but I never said a word. He had intruded on my newfound world.

As a child I had an enormous inner need to identify with something, to connect. I was subconsciously probing. I found school not only not answering my needs, but utterly boring. I could not succumb to that kind of regimentation, so I sought ways to escape. Yet I had a passion for learning, born of my own being, my feeling-center, which craved expression. I needed to know if there was someone else who felt as I did, which would confirm and validate my own sense of self. Children invariably question their intuition when confronted with negative, regimented, unyielding patterns. "What's wrong with me?" they ask. "Why do I feel this way? Am I the only one who feels like this? Why does this feeling persist?" Then at some point they either succumb to society, or they break free to continue their search for self, for truth, and for their own being.

LOOKING FOR TRAGEDY

Negativity has become so all-pervasive that many people are disappointed if I give them a reading and don't include tragedy. "How long will I live?" "When will I be sick?" they ask. Instead of asking what the good things are in their future and what their possibilities are, they expect tragedy and sadness. Then they are surprised when their expectations are fulfilled.

In readings there are times when certain traumatic events are projected, yet that too has its purpose. Even a seeming tragedy can be approached from a creative point of view. Often it is indicated that a relative is about to pass on, but that the relationship between the relative and the person being read is one of fear, mistrust, or lack of communication. Instead, this is an opportunity for the subject to know that the particular relative is not going to be around much longer. There is still a chance to work out a resolution within the relationship, before the opportunity is lost in this lifespan.

The subject has to utilize this opportunity and work out whatever it is that necessitated the relationship with his particular mother, father, brother, or sister. What has not been corrected in a previous life must be faced all over again, either in this lifetime or a subsequent one. While we're here we have a prime opportunity to resolve our difficulties, and we must seize the moment while our loved ones are still in this life. The urgency ought to be overwhelming as we resolve every relationship with one another, in love and harmony, to discover ourselves anew. Our new greatness, capacity, and potential is heightened, thereby creating new realities.

In this way, I deal positively with certain seemingly tragic projections. To me, a reading has to be on the constructive side. Something creative has to come out of it whereby the subject emerges with a new point of view. We are all gifted. We all have latent talents. We simply need direction, encouragement, and confirmation.

No matter how much we see, there's always something larger than what we are currently seeing in our lives that we want to awaken to. This applies to anyone, wherever they are in life, no matter how realized they are. It's never a matter of reaching a point and saying, "Look! I've arrived!" There is no such thing. There is always something we have yet to glimpse and this is what makes life so fascinating.

The difficult thing for people to grasp is that no matter what situation they are in, they have attracted it into their own lives, whether they are consciously aware of it or not. That's a hard thing to face. We always allocate so much power to external conditions in life. We rarely say, "*Why* has it happened to *me* and not to somebody else?" This should always be at the heart of our thinking: "Whatever is happening is happening to me, so by necessity I must consider the whys. Why have I attracted it into my life?" We have to realize the heavy hand we've had in attracting every experience. Having done that, we're in a better position to desire change in ourselves.

Once you can identify yourself as the one responsible for having created your own experiences, then you are in a wonderful position to change. Only then can you realize that *you don't have to stay where you are.*

An intelligent woman came to see me for a reading. Because she began to relive all her past traumatic experiences, she went through a box of tissues, crying as she revived her most painful memories. She did not realize how instrumental she had been in scripting her life. She described to me her childhood and her difficulties with her parents. To make her point stronger, she added that she wasn't the only one to suffer. Her brothers and sisters were under the same influence. She felt so justified in her hatred toward her parents; she held onto her anger, harboring each grudge and allowing her bitterness to completely stop her from enjoying her life. As long as she held onto these past things and allowed them to dictate to her today, giving them power, she wasn't going to get anywhere. She couldn't relate to another human being; as things stood she had nothing to give. None of her extensive knowledge and abilities could nourish her soul.

The reading indicated the possibilities that stood in front of her, and how she could free herself from all the hatred and guilt if only she would look at it from a larger perspective. She (and her brothers and sisters) had attracted their problems into their lives for karmic reasons. Now, if she chose, she could move on and free herself; she would no longer have to remain stuck.

She was an intellectual woman, but there's a big difference between knowledge and wisdom. We put so much importance on degrees given by universities; the intellect gets so highly developed that it becomes our greatest enemy, as far as our eternal life is concerned.

People are constantly searching, but in their search they are misled by the dictates of society. What is right today may be wrong tomorrow. Such is the fickleness of mass-thinking. Psychiatry is currently fashionable and respectable. Today you don't even have to be neurotic because the most normal person supposedly can benefit from psychiatric care. But look at psychiatry. It mostly deals with past hurts and traumas, wrongs inflicted on the patient—in short, blaming others. And what does the patient do with this material, dredged up from the depths of the past and the deeper impressions of the formative years? The patient begins to choke on it by reliving and regurgitating material that no longer holds any value in life today.

Primarily, psychiatry is busy unearthing material that is no longer relevant. It rarely deals with the person in the *now*. Instead, it justifies the past and gives power to dead matter.

As long as psychiatry continues in this manner, it cannot be anything but detrimental for the patient.

To dig up some particular experience from your childhood is not enough. If you're going to do that, you'd have to dig up all your childhoods; you'd have to go through all your past lives. The premise of psychiatry is wrong, because it cannot effect real change. Yet there are times when seeming changes occur for people under psychiatric care, but these changes are mostly modifications.

Then the patient becomes dangerously dependent on his doctor. It's another way of being hooked; it's another habit, another crutch—and much easier than being on your own because you don't have to assume responsibility for yourself. How often have you heard someone say, "I see my shrink. He tells me I'm justified in my feelings of anger, so I give him a hundred bucks. It's worth it to me. I feel better."

No price is too high for one's own justification. Clearly, psychiatry is still in its infancy. But more and more therapists are beginning to work with patients from a spiritual background—their dreams, past lives, a recognition of the eternal in us. Psychiatrists have as much to learn from their patients as teachers do from their pupils.

LOOK AT YOURSELF

Recently I was paid a visit by a man whom I've known for many years. He has had a great many challenges in his personal life. About two years ago, he became involved in a certain kind of "self-improvement" philosophy and it has altered his life.

He called on me to explain the wonders of this particular group and their techniques for dealing with life. Later the conversation got around to his niece, and he began to tell me how lost she was. The girl had become a member of another religious cult claiming their own answers to life, and she was trying to convert him to her new beliefs.

How quickly we latch onto a new authority and how fervently we try to shove it down someone else's throat. It's so easy to get lost in a noble cause, the perfect excuse not to look at ourselves. We want so desperately to avoid ourselves, to be distracted with magic potions and instant solutions. Our lives are staring us in the face, but we don't want to really examine ourselves because that would involve us directly—and then we would have to do something about it. So we allow ourselves to be blinded by other people's supposed illumination.

This is one of the reasons why groups and churches and mass gatherings are so popular. People always feel safer in numbers. It's another excuse not to equate with the self, to escape the self in a noble, acceptable, honorable way, because hundreds or thousands of others are doing it. "I belong, I attend, I'm a member. It's wonderful. Look what we're doing for others." It becomes the *we* instead of the I— and that's literally mass-thinking at work!

There's always the desire to belong to a group; if we all vibrate together, it's supposedly more dynamic. But where are your own dynamics? Your energies come from your own inner being, not from someone else. Only *you* can pull yourself out of where you're at. You've got to learn to be your own messiah.

One of the most common hindrances to self-development is equating with the mind of another, be it a group, church, or individual. They would have you believe that what others are doing is wrong, what others are saying is wrong, and what others believe is wrong. I have a relative who is always counting everybody's money. Now it certainly doesn't make me any richer if I count your money, nor is it going to make me any better if I count all your wrongs. But it's this kind of thinking with which many people and groups are preoccupied.

It's much easier to see the wrongs in others; it's much more difficult to see them in ourselves. Notice what bothers you about another person. That is exactly what you dislike most in yourself! In my work, even the seemingly negative things are rewarding since I continually learn from them. Inevitably, all exchanges with supposed strangers come to mirror an aspect of myself. You meet yourself over and over again in everyone you encounter.

As a child I was fascinated by Russian authors. They are so dramatic, so deeply perceptive of human nature, and so very sad. I believe it was Pushkin who tells the following story.

During the time of the Tsars, the military was the elite class and everyone else was unimportant. A certain little nobody boards a train for Moscow and sharing his compartment is a famous general, bedecked with medals. The poor little man sneezes, and of course his saliva hits the distinguished general's medals. Trembling, he begins to apologize. Immediately the general dismisses the incident, but the little fellow is frantic with guilt. His shame and embarrassment are overwhelming. The distinction he has created between himself and the general is so acute that he goes out and kills himself.

Now you might say that this story is carried to the extreme, but this is truly an excellent example of human behavior. The little man couldn't forgive himself, and this is true of all of us—we do not forgive ourselves. It's not a matter of someone else forgiving us. It is to the extent that you can forgive yourself that you can free and rid yourself of your guilt patterns. Then and only then can you begin to live in freedom. Your life is totally dependent on your own forgiveness, and to the extent that we can forgive ourselves, can we then begin to forgive others.

People are forever short-changing themselves. They think so little of themselves. Our acceptability to ourselves is something that really needs to be examined. We always seek out others to tell us how wonderful we are, and for that moment we're inspired: "Gee, I'm great." But pretty soon we think otherwise, and that inspiration becomes meaningless. Unless you can find the answer within yourself, learn how to accept yourself, there is nothing that can be told or given or taught that will make any lasting difference.

A woman who came to me expressed a deep desire to be married, yet did everything in her talking and feeling to eliminate the possibility. She acted out the very opposite of what she desired. As the reading continued, she became analytical and cold. "Well, I guess marriage is not for me," she declared. Minutes later she justified it even further by saying, "I suppose marriage is not for everyone. There are other things in life; being married is not that important."'

Throughout her reading, marriage was indicated as the most important factor in her life. As it increased in importance and frequency in the reading, she finally allowed herself to be honest and admit to her inner feelings. Still, wanting to save pride, she felt compelled to utter, "But I guess it's up to me. I chase them away."

What she was doing was rejecting *herself*, to *herself*, rather than face rejection from a man. Out of fear she withdrew from life. There are all kinds of withdrawals. We can withdraw from the outside world in contemplation or inner creativity. Or we can withdraw from life, as she had done, to escape reality and stew over our hurts and failures.

As we talked, she began to see that she had retreated in fear of being hurt; therefore, she had surrounded herself with conjured justifications. When she left, she had a new image of herself. She saw the real possibility of marriage, akin to her inner feelings—rather than the hopelessness with which she had equated for so long. She now realized the choice was hers to make.

Once a person sees her symptoms, once her patterns are apparent, she can look and handle herself with far greater understanding. Our symptoms are our mirror, and that mirror is staring at us all the time. Once you know this, you are inspired to do something about it. Desire motivates you in a new direction.

How can you tell when you're negative? How do you know when you're on the wrong path in life? You should certainly be able to discern that very easily. If you are walking stooped over, you are certainly not exhilarating in life. If you are thinking of death all the time, you are certainly not being positive. If you are preoccupied with physical ailments, you are certainly not equating with health. If you have headaches, backaches, if your legs are swollen, if your neck is wrenched—you have evidence of your state of negativity. Lingering negativities result in even deeper discomforts.

For each of us, the signals may be slightly different, but they are unmistakable when you learn to recognize them. After a while, as you watch and observe, you will find that everyone has his own pet peeves, his own symptoms. With some people it's sneezing, with others headaches or upset stomachs, but it is an appropriate group of symptoms that occurs in our negative states in a pattern unique to each person.

Look at yourself. Watch your signals. If they're negative, immediately set to work to determine what is wrong. Now you must declare its opposite, from a negative to a positive. That reverses the process—all you have to do is shift your attention, and you will find energy working for you rather than against you. Make the positive your new reality.

Habitually, because of our upbringing, we have accepted these negative patterns as truth. When anything new is introduced to us, we automatically say No or resist, and that is definitely a negative. Try saying Yes. Try turning it about. Yes opens doors. No shuts them. By reversing the process, you open something in you that was closed previously. Why not? Whether it's a dinner invitation or a new thought, at least think about it. You never know where a door will lead you.

Everything co-exists within us, negative and positive, and this is where we need to make our selection. In order not to remain in duality, it is important to select that which is helpful in your life, that which is inspiring in you, that which generates the creativity of your own inner resources. In order to do that, you must *still the intellect*, which tends to be argumentative about everything.

There is a story about a man in search of God. In his travels he meets many gurus, and each of them gives him a different piece of advice. The first guru says, "If you habitually get out of bed on the right-hand side, try getting out of bed on the left-hand side." He tries it for a while without results. Another guru says, "You must get rid of all your possessions." He does, but it doesn't work for him. A third guru says he must renounce his family. He does that, too, but he still doesn't discover God.

Finally he gets to the highest mountain in the Himalayas, where he finds the oldest, wisest guru of them all. He relates all his searching and tribulations and his failure. The old and wise guru says, "You have searched in all the wrong places. God is within you."

The man is angered and argues, "But I've looked everywhere and I've done everything and still I have not found God. There is no such thing!"

The old guru ponders this and after a long pause shakes his head ruefully and says, "You mean to tell me there really is no God?"

❧ CHAPTER THREE ❧

WAKE UP—YOU ARE ALIVE!

If your life were to be spent on a precipice, in constant danger, and you could not move, it would be better to live in that way than not to live at all.

AN EIGHTY-SEVEN-YEAR-OLD WOMAN

Even though I am in the position of writing this book, I am also the recipient of constant lessons. An eighty-seven-year-old widow came to me once for a reading. As I looked at her, I thought, "What in the world could I possibly tell her?" Then I mentally kicked myself. "Who are you to judge? She's here for a reason. Sit down and do your thing!"

Soon it was indicated that there was a man who was very interested in her. She also cared for him a great deal. Finally, I threw away the cards and asked, "Well, why don't you marry him?"

She looked me straight in the eye and replied, "What's my hurry?"

That was one of the most beautiful, refreshing things I ever heard. I sat up and truly looked at her. I had been judging her dead, and she was very much alive. It was a good lesson for me. Later she told me she was being wined and dined and taken everywhere by him. Eventually, I learned they had gotten married.

Unconsciously we all place so much importance on time. We have no idea how much of it penetrates into our lives. It is the quality of life we need concern ourselves with, not the worrying about time running out. Then we discover that we have all the time in the world; we simply need to clear our thinking and know it! By keeping a reverence for life toward everything we encounter, we dissolve time. We have received the greatest gift of all—our lives. By using this gift constructively, lovingly, every moment becomes precious and time becomes meaningless.

GURDJIEFF, KRISHNAMURTI, CAYCE, AND BARKER

All my life I have been searching—perhaps not consciously knowing what I was searching for. Every time I found something I felt possibly held the answer for me, it merely intensified my search.

I had a friend who was a member of a Gurdjieff study group. Over a period of a year or so, my husband and I were invited to her home regularly, where there was always a group of people, and a "teacher," so to speak. I thought members of the group were all friends of hers, as it all appeared to be social, but I later discovered that we were being scrutinized as possible members of their circle. When my friend finally brought the subject up, I was furious with her; she had known me for years and knew very well that I had always been interested in philosophy and religion.

I had to write letters saying why my husband and I wanted to join the group. We had to read certain books and explain what they meant to us. Finally, we were admitted as members. The meetings always began with ten minutes of silence, during which my husband fell asleep immediately. He snored quite loudly, but the others always accepted it— after all, showing tolerance was a sign of evolvement.

A few months later, I began to feel that the whole Gurdjieff organization was very limiting. There was a hierarchy of officers, the important people; and then came the little people. The higher-ups would verbally browbeat individuals in order to extract something from them, to get them to talk. The manner in which it was conducted bothered me. I have always had a thirst for inner knowledge and inner growth. I still want to find out so much. But with this particular group I was continually being restricted. They were forever putting you down rather than communicating anything. We were all there to gain something about ourselves, but we were cut off again and again. Everything was at the convenience of the hierarchy, who were caught up with their own importance, and thereby meted out how much one was allowed to savor. Moreover, you could not attend certain meetings because the hierarchy judged whether you were advanced enough.

There came a time when I was preparing for an extended trip, which was to include England for three months, where the Gurdjieff organization has its headquarters. I went up to the leader of my local group and explained that I was going to be in England and would like to join some of the activities there. She turned to me and icily snarled, "Who in hell do you think you are?"

Needless to say, I was not granted permission to participate in London. But my trip also took me to Switzerland, where I was to join a seminar led by Krishnamurti. He was there every summer in Saanen, outside of Gstaad, giving lectures in a huge tent. I had read almost everything he had written and was very excited about going.

After his second lecture, I sat down and wrote a letter of resignation to my Gurdjieff group leader. It was fifteen pages long, and I expressed my feelings very honestly. In the letter I used comparisons about knowledge. If you have something, you can't hold it back. If someone is thirsting for what you have, and you don't respond, then you are operating under a completely false premise. I later discovered my letter became a manifesto in the Gurdjieff group. It was their topic for three months! It was studied; I was analyzed from top to bottom; and naturally the verdict was that there was something wrong with me, certainly not with them. They really couldn't understand my quitting and long afterward were coaxing me to return.

I then became very deeply involved with the philosophy of Krishnamurti. I returned to Switzerland the following summer and was thinking of going to India, where he did most of his work. He moved freely and wasn't connected with any group, and I liked that. The people who traveled with him did so directly out of their own rather than his desire.

As I started preparing to spend a year in India with him, in a program he was giving at that time, I came to think of myself as a specially chosen person, which, I began to believe, necessitated giving up my personal life.

It is a dangerous trap to think of yourself as nominated to do a great work for humanity, and I had fallen into it. I was strongly influenced by Krishnamurti, and I felt myself changing. Somehow, when I came back to my husband and our marriage after that first summer in Saanen, I was no longer the person I had been before I left. My husband's need for the marriage at that time was so great, however, that I felt guilty for even thinking of ending it. He was willing to sacrifice anything and everything if we would only stay together. So I never went to India.

I had begun to fall asleep in my marriage and yet I couldn't muster enough strength to follow Krishnamurti. I was undecided and staying home was the easy way out. Not having left the marriage, and no longer entertaining the illusion that I was a chosen person, my disappointment and letdown were so intense that I almost ceased functioning. I went through all the mechanics of being a wife, but my heart and my feelings had gone back into slumberland. It was then that I found a book by Edgar Cayce. Another door sprung open.

Soon afterward I attended two seminars on dreams at

the Edgar Cayce Foundation in Virginia Beach. Upon my return I formed a Cayce group with some friends. I was off again. But that was short-lived, too. Whenever people start meeting regularly under the guise of a search, it eventually becomes trivialized and diluted. Groups create dependency and give a false sense of belonging. Social considerations take over and the essential work becomes secondary.

Some more time slipped by, until I heard of Dr. Raymond Barker, whose Religious Science headquarters are in New York City. I attended a few of his lectures and was very impressed with him. It seemed to me that he was showing people the tools to work with, tools which they could apply in their own lives. Barker talked of certain things that had produced definite results. And I was ready for results.

I studied with Dr. Barker for two years. He taught the necessity of applying that which you knew. I had been talking and intellectualizing. Now it was time for action. But I soon discovered I could only apply what I had come to understand to myself and my daughters. I couldn't apply it to my marriage.

Then one day my husband left me. Surprisingly, it was the shock of my life. If there was one thought I had never entertained, it was the possibility that he would walk out on me. I was on my own for the first time in years. Suddenly I had to cope, and I didn't know where to start. He had always taken care of everything. I didn't even know how much the mortgage payment was. Now I was forced to face the realities of everyday living, and that was what really woke me up. Only then did I realize how long I had been asleep.

The first thing I said to myself (and later repeated over and over again) was "Grace, it's the best thing that ever happened to you." I could share this view with only one close friend who was on the same wavelength. She agreed immediately and often repeated the thought back to me. But other friends, when they heard what had happened, came to offer solace and sympathy. Even though my heart was aching, I found myself calming them by flippantly saying, "Well, look at it this way. It's not that I lost a husband, I've gained an extra closet."

CHANGE IS THE TRUE REALITY

We all seek security, something to hold on to. We don't like to be shaken up. We want everything to be permanent and there is no such thing, really. We fear change, which is in fact the only constant reality. Change is inevitable, necessary, and wonderful not only in terms of the external point of view but, far more important, from an internal point of life also. We're never the same, even from one second to the next. And thank God for that!

We never look at anything the same way for very long, our viewpoint continually changes. Even when contemplating God, and reflecting on our relationship to God, our conception tomorrow will be different from what it is today. We are forever unfolding, growing from our experiences. And as we grow by necessity we change. We gain deeper insight, deeper understanding. With it comes new projections and different ways of looking at things.

Nothing is that firmly steadfast or stationary—*nothing*. This is where we falter, because we want everything to be permanent, in order to fit into something we can grasp and hold on to.

There's an old adage that goes: "Never throw away the dirty water until you have clean water." Well, how in the world are you going to put clean water in a pail when it's still full of dirty water? You've got to empty it first in order to make room for the clean water. That's the kind of total job that has to be done on our thinking. You can't do it halfway.

What is required is a thorough spiritual house-cleaning, and that is not easy. We cling to what we think we know. We are frightened of that which we don't know. We project from our assumed knowing into regions we know nothing about, and this produces terrible fear. We take our past fears (which were bad enough by themselves) and project them into a future possibility, which can only result in more fear. We're always completely misusing our "now" time by not being here *in* the "now." We're either in the past with our fears, or we're projecting a future based on those very fears. Not only do we misuse the now, we're not even here. Mostly we're in the *there* and *then*. When you can decondition yourself, and learn to accept change and not-knowing as beautiful possibilities, the loosening up process begins. You start to free yourself, and this letting go of the past becomes the difference between freedom and captivity.

But how many people are inwardly ready to totally shed all their preconceptions, all their preconditioning? Total detachment is a very difficult thing in the personality we assume in this life; it is an enormous task. Yet we must all come to it sooner or later, if not in this life, in subsequent ones. We have to come to it eventually.

We must demolish most of the foundations that we falsely rest on in order to erect a new structure, and that necessitates radical annihilation. Anything else is a modification, a false premise.

A total transformation of self cannot be forced. It comes about through giving in, letting go. Acquiescing, rather than opposing. Accepting, rather than resisting. Not just passive acceptance—but acceptance with enthusiasm. We can never afford to lose our enthusiasm. If we are in step with life, we are naturally enthusiastic.

SENSING YOURSELF

Before retiring for the night, take five minutes to go over your activities of the day. It's been a wonderful day, no matter how good or bad it was. There was a lot of material that was not useful—discard it. There were many situations that you handled very well—give thanks for them. Yet you know you can improve, so mentally review in what way you could have better managed these things. Then next time, in similar experiences, you may add that extra warmth, attention, kindness, and love that might have been lacking the day before. Now you are done with the day, finished. You are ready for a good night's rest, in communication with your subconscious mind.

Upon awakening, you're ready to greet the day with your own newness. You will be as new to the day as the day is to you. Before you do anything else, take another five minutes to be with yourself. Establish contact with your inner resources, your own awareness. Then, as you go through your day's activities, you have your center to refer to, to come back to, if you find yourself slipping back into old habits, behaving like an automaton.

These two brief periods of contact with your inner being will begin to heighten your awareness of yourself. Stay with your newfound center. It is not important what other people are thinking. We're much too preoccupied with what other people are doing or saying. The mass tendency is to attend to everybody else's business and leave our own business unattended. You have to work on yourself. You have to do your own equating and your own reckoning. You can't afford to take anyone's word as law, or accept anyone's attitude as your own. Your only reference is self. You need to become like a detective: Observe what's going on inside of you, every detail and inclination. It's a full-time job—so much so that you won't have time to enter into other people's business.

Once contact is established with your inner being, the implementation of your new program will stretch beyond the five senses. The inner and outer world come into harmony. With inner rapport, we can create a purposeful world for ourselves. The collective progress of society is very slow, sometimes taking centuries before change is apparent. In your own life, you can supersede all. There's no limit to your rate of acceleration. You can move very rapidly in your own growth. Through that togetherness within self, you become a contributing factor to the world at large. But never when you are separated within yourself. When disharmony reigns, you're of little value to yourself or to anyone else.

Togetherness within the self can only come through awareness—through the unification of the conscious and the subconscious mind. What is the constant war going on within us? It's the spirit beckoning one thing and the conscious mind fighting it, intellectualizing it away. Unless these two forces come together, you're in big trouble, and you'll encounter one mishap after another.

It's remarkable what we can do, how powerful we are—when we let go. Most people don't know what I mean by that. "I have all these problems; how can I let go?" they ask. Well, the first thing to get rid of is the *how*. It's the *hows*, the *buts*, the *whys* that are the obstacles to your growth.

First of all, you have to sense yourself, and you can only sense yourself in deeper ways if you let go of your habitual thinking and start to pay attention to your inner being. The most difficult thing you can undertake is to *let go*; to let go of that little self called ego. You feel as if you're losing ground and are no longer in charge of your life. The, ego must be abandoned, because it always interferes and keeps you from getting to the truth. That "how?" is always your ego asking, delaying you from getting to the heart of the matter. Abandoning the ego is the one thing we fear the most—*because we have come to believe that that is all we are.* Yet in order to sense yourself in a higher way, and discover your true being, ego must go.

MEDITATION

The closest we can come in contact to God is in meditation. In meditating, you are in touch with your subconscious mind directly. Meditation is your direct line to the higher intelligence. Truly meditating, of course, not simply daydreaming.

Set aside a certain time daily; select a quiet spot; sit in silence. Shut out the external world. Relax yourself so totally that you're no longer aware of your body. Empty your mind, still the intellect. This is step one, this type of meditation, of abandoning the ego. Relax and let go. Random thoughts will rush in; observe them and throw them out. At first you need to start this way to deliberately shut out the material world. Soon you'll sense yourself as part of a direct current—you and your relationship to God. It is the closest we can come to communion between ourselves and the infinite intelligence.

What is necessary here is a degree of regularity and a certain discipline. The subconscious mind can only be impressed through repetition; the more silent you become, the louder it hears you. So whatever approach you use, you have to repeat it. If it helps you to remove attention from self by focusing on a candle flame, good, but that may not work for another. For someone else, the lotus position may be desirable. Or perhaps sitting straight in a chair without falling asleep, maintaining alertness, but at the same time suspending the body. For everyone it is something different. You have to find your own key, your own mode.

Once found, it must be repeated regularly, again and again, so the subconscious mind knows you mean business. Through repetition, rapport is established. Later on, you can loosen the ritual. You will find yourself able to meditate anywhere—in a crowd, a bus, at work, parties, wherever. Soon you'll no longer be restricted to an exact time or place.

But at first you'll have to discipline yourself. This comes with the desire to reach your goal, to reach God. That desire is your inspiration. You entertain that desire in your own imagination as the possibility of becoming and unfolding. As you realize that you are much more than you believe yourself to be, the desire to make discoveries about yourself is the single most exciting experience there is! Any meditation is a way to begin discovering more and more of yourself in relationship to God.

Practice shutting out the world for ten minutes every

day. Let go of everything that distracts you in your daily activity. You don't realize how much influence these distractions have, constantly going on around you and through you.

When I first came to this country, my aunt met me at the pier and we took a cab to her home. The moment we got in the taxi I'll never forget how the cabby performed three actions simultaneously: he turned the radio on, blasting; he asked our destination, shouting; and he lit a cigar, smelling! All this was done unconsciously, automatically, and instantaneously. I remember marveling to myself, "How incredible!"

We distract ourselves repeatedly from ourselves, from our beautiful inner selves. To demonstrate the wisdom of life, take time out, be quiet. Still yourself and know that you are God.

"I Am"

Another way to get to know your inner self is to talk to yourself. For a whole month try saying nothing but "I am" silently, no matter what you encounter. Exciting things will come through you in a positive way that will help you discover yourself. "I am" to everything. "I am" to everyone. "I am"—even if you're being hit on the head.

"I am" makes you sit up straight and take notice of your being. When you are in the "I am" you can't possibly be worrying. Instead of being consumed with your problems, reverse the process; and make it "I am. I can feel myself; I can sense myself; I'm alive. I am!" If you bring that into action as a beginning, another creative approach to the self is found, another road. "I am" will wake you up and heighten your awareness. Nonsense you formerly considered so important will no longer matter.

After you've done "I am" for a good month, and have made some beautiful discoveries about yourself, you're ready to attach something to it. "I am wonderful." "I am great." "I am beautiful." At first, you may hear yourself making these statements and feel ridiculous. But do it anyway. Verbalize it.

One day something will click, and suddenly you realize you are unique, you are wonderful, and you are no longer laughing at yourself, because now you have discovered your own truth. You begin to *feel* something unique about yourself, and it fits. You have become the thing itself. When you say "I am wonderful" you have simply extracted a truth about yourself.

This will be difficult at first. Some people may come to me, for instance, and their physical discomfort will project itself right away in the reading. I will stop for a moment and direct their attention to the "I am" and then introduce health as a concept. I will have them repeat it out loud: "I am health." And their reaction is usually embarrassment, as they choke on the words, because people identify so much with sickness. Usually women more so, because it's their subject for conversation—"Let me tell you about my operation"—it's an attention-getter. Whereas men generally identify far more with health.

But recently I had two young men come for a reading. They were both under twenty, and each of them asked me, "What about my health? You didn't tell me I was going to be sick, and when." Look how they program themselves! As if everyone, at some point in their lives, has to have an illness! When you find this attitude in young people, you can immediately detect the influence they're under in their home environment. This is not the young person talking but rather parents talking through them. They have not yet questioned enough about life and have merely accepted these falsehoods blindly, without experimentation. "What about my health?" they asked. So, I replied, "What *about* your health?"

Right after them came a woman with the same attitude. It was a cycle that day. Immediately it was indicated that she had a great deal wrong with her physically, although of

✿ CHAPTER FIVE ✿

DREAMS ARE OUR FOOD

*The majority of your dreams are direct
messages to you; they are your connections
with the spirit-world.*

THE DREAMING PROCESS

There is an inner being, an inner sensing in us that responds—not to logic, but to the illogical. It is a feeling that
can't be rationalized, an intuitive feeling that really links
you with a sense of continuity to your past lives.

This brings us to memories. Certainly it isn't the conscious mind that remembers the dream process, but feelings
that persist without logical explanation. In order to unify
conscious and subconscious mind, these feelings play themselves out in your dream-life. There they can become intelli-
gible to you.

A dream takes place on many different levels of the
mind. In a very deep sleep you are in touch with the
superconscious mind where the dream originates. The
dream symbology of the superconscious mind is totally unfamiliar to the conscious mind, there is a mediator—the subconscious mind—which translates the dream into a form
that you, the dreamer, can learn to understand. Otherwise,
in its original state, the conscious mind could never understand the dream form as first projected by the superconscious mind.

Next, you enter a shallower level of sleep, in which the conscious mind is ready to receive the message. Subconscious mind has already done the interpretation and is now delivering the symbology to the conscious mind in a more accessible way—so that the conscious mind can work with it. The subconscious mind *knows* and endeavors to trigger the memory of the conscious mind.

Even with this mediator, the symbology appears to the dreamer as hieroglyphics. At this level, the symbology is still something of a puzzle, if you're not familiar with it feelingly. But the material is within your grasp. It is translatable and decipherable.

Studied from an intelligent, sensible point of view, you can understand the function of each symbol that appears in your dream. A hand, for instance. Ask yourself: "What does a hand perform?" You have to associate the object with its function and then connect it with the feelings you experience within the dream because your feelings play a very important part. In this way you begin to intelligently apply every part of the dream to yourself.

REMEMBERING AND CONNECTING DREAMS

Have you ever noticed how active and vivid a dream-life children experience? And how fewer and fewer dreams are remembered in adulthood? The actual dreams do not diminish, they still go on. But children, being in an all subconscious state, are totally in touch with the spirit-world they have just come from. Dreams are the world of reality for children, their home. This planet Earth is foreign ground to them.

Dream experiences should be no less vivid when we grow up—but as adults we turn away from the dream dimension of existence, and deliberately, consciously, shut it out. Through the continuing adjustment to society, and the mass-thinking that nothing in dreams is true or has any merit, we focus totally on the material world and shut out the memory of our dreams. But dreams go on, for everybody, at whatever level of consciousness we may be.

The quality, significance, and meaning of dreams vary in accordance with our individual level of consciousness. The dreaming process is continual whether the conscious mind accepts the messages or not.

Children let their dreams flow, without hang-ups, unless confronted by parents who tell them, "Dreams are all nonsense. Pay no attention to them." Under this kind of influence, children soon shut the doors to their dream reality. When parents discourage this natural expression, the child begins to falter. "Maybe there's something wrong with me," he thinks. Through this impression on the subconscious mind, the child will consciously try not to remember dreams.

This leads us to remembering past lives and how to connect your dreams to yourself. Through dream form we make our first connection. For the most part, dreams are your soul's way of communicating with your conscious self. They alert the conscious self to a spiritual dimension whence the dream originates. Remembering your dreams upon awakening serves as a reminder of your connection to a higher realm.

A friend told me that he frequently has very uncomfortable, unpleasant dreams, but he cannot remember them when he awakens. It's quite clear that he doesn't want to remember what he is experiencing. In his case it probably has to do with a past incarnation which must have been very painful, and he doesn't want these memories to surface. He's simply not ready for them. If he were, the memory of the dreams would be forthcoming. Just as we can hypnotize ourselves into remembering and understanding our dreams while the dream is taking place, we can just as easily hypnotize ourselves into *not wanting to remember* our dreams. The same principle is at work. The conscious mind shuts out the dreams; it wants to remain disconnected; it doesn't want to confront anything or make any effort toward self-improvement and resolution.

To more clearly recall your dreams, put yourself in a state of receptivity by sleeping with your head north. It takes twenty times more energy to sleep with your body aligned east-west than aligned north-south. By sleeping north-south, you are in harmony with the Earth's magnetic poles and better prepared to remember your dreams.

Next, remind your subconscious that you are ready to receive your dreams, and that you want to consciously remember them. Before going to bed each night, make contact with the subconscious. Tell it emphatically: "I want to remember my dreams when I awaken." This has to be done regularly, every night, especially by those who consistently do not remember their dreams. Be ready with pencil and paper nearby to write down your dreams no matter when you awaken, even in the middle of the night.

If you're serious enough and stay with it, the subconscious will begin to trigger your memory. The more you work with your dreams and their messages, the more acutely the dreams will become available. We have eight to ten dreams a night, whether we remember them or not. We cannot afford to miss a single one of them. Their communications are vital to our wholeness and enlightenment.

With practice you'll begin remembering your dreams and connect them more meaningfully with your day-to-day life. As you heighten the connection between conscious and subconscious mind, you are ready to autosuggest the *resolution* during the dream itself. The reverse is true in your waking life. Your conscious mind can autosuggest resolutions that the subconscious mind will deliver. In a sense it's an hypnotic influence, be it self-hypnosis or any other form of mesmerizing. Just as you hypnotize your subconscious with demands from your conscious being, in a subconscious state you can hypnotize yourself further into knowing what to extract from a particular dream.

In sleep, the body is relaxed; the conscious mind is totally out of the way; you're in a suspended state, a kind of trance-receivership. Even in that state there is still something retained in you from your conscious reality which can direct the subconscious mind to bring your dream into explanation and even into resolve.

We can perfect ourselves in any state of reality. We do it all the time by hypnotizing ourselves in one form or another. The valuable work we can do for our own growth and understanding in this lifetime is the exciting part: You can resolve every problem, every aspect which deals with yourself and your life in your dreams.

In your subconscious state you can hypnotize your conscious mind and bring your entire being into unity. Having gone that far, to where you can now resolve your problems within your dreams, you are no longer dependent on symbols or details. You can take the dream form even further— into the superconscious state, where the dream originates, where the soul actually triggers the dream into existence. Once the other two minds are in unison you can move toward a direct wire to the superconscious. Now you can take it to the source. When you have done that, you no longer have to dream at all.

Sleep Is Soul-Travel

In sleep, when the conscious mind is out of the way at night, we dream and the soul travels. The moment you fall asleep—even for a few minutes—your soul is off. Based on your development, it travels through different dimensions; not only from planet to planet, but back through all your past incarnations.

We have spent much more time traveling in space than in all our repeated lives here on Earth, and therefore we are far more familiar with our beings in the spirit-world where our true sense of belonging is felt. When we sleep, we're constantly traveling. That's why you should always awaken others gently, never harshly. You need to give them a chance for the soul to come back into their body. Suppose you are having a dream and you can't orient yourself immediately; you're on foreign territory. If someone were to startle you awake, it would have a very adverse effect, because you'd be disoriented *there* and disoriented *here*. You'd be unable to assimilate either reality. There is always the fear, on an unconscious level, of not having enough time to get back into the body. In your dream state you know you have enough time. Any outside interference, however, triggers the fear of not getting back.

The soul travels very fast, beyond any conception we have of time or speed. To be awakened suddenly creates an emergency situation, and the soul has to go even faster than its normal speed.

Most important, it has not completed its journey and returned of its own accord. By breaking off its experiencing elsewhere and rushing back into this physical reality, a shock is rendered to the whole system, especially the heart. The soul has been journeying in timelessness, but the interruption comes to impose time, and the soul has to comply with earthly laws. Sometimes the soul does not make it back, and this is why some people have heart attacks in their sleep.

There is an ongoing nourishment that we receive while reviewing our past lives, which is an integral part of our being here. To be rudely awakened can *cut off your connection* between all worlds—the dream-world, this world, the spirit-world, and any dimension the soul moves through. It takes awhile to get your bearings, and even then there is still a sense of something missing, something incomplete, which is unbalancing.

This phenomenon of soul-travel is quite evident in babies, who are totally subconscious mind and therefore continually traveling. They are still fresh to their surroundings here. The slightest touch is startling, the slightest noise will disturb them. You must always be soft and gentle, to give them a chance to acquaint themselves with this world, letting them know it's a safe, loving place.

Many people, particularly children, dream repeatedly about falling and often awaken in terror. Falling into space, into a hole, into nothingness is actually a flight experience. They are truly experiencing the sensation of the soul traveling, falling back into its body, returning to its physical home. The sensation is always frightening because the conscious mind cannot fully comprehend.

Sleepwalking is another form of being in between two worlds. A sleepwalker is actually acting out what is experienced in another dimension, and one wants to be gentle and careful in dealing with them. No harm can come to a sleepwalker, because she or he is completely protected by subconscious mind. You will find sleepwalking takes place mostly in children and is very rare among adults. Children are still largely under the influence of where they were prior to their incarnation on Earth. They are acquainted with that dimension far more than this present plane of life. No matter how many times we have reincarnated on Earth this dimension is fairly new to us.

All transitions are difficult, whether the adjustment be from Earth experience into spirit-world, or from spirit-world into an Earth experience. Some people get their bearings far better than others. Those who have incarnated a great many more times may possibly have an easier adjustment period than others. The more you connect things now, the easier all transitions become.

What Is Déjà Vu?

In the dream-reality nothing seems fantastic to the dreamer. We're never amazed by the symbology. We accept the most implausible things as commonplace and routine. In dreams, we cannot project anything that does not exist, as remote as that may seem to the conscious mind. There is not a symbol, an idea, a thought, a feeling, that does not bear out the truth, its own reality or existence. This is because a dream has to travel through you, the receiver, and the material must first exist at some level or else you could not conceive of it.

Probably all of us at one time or another have had an experience of déjà vu. But what really is déjà vu? It's something already glimpsed, something familiar, something seen before or previously experienced. But where have you seen it? Where does it come from? Where have you experienced it? In memory. In dreams.

The greatest revelations we receive are in dream form first, whether in the sleep state or in the altered consciousness state, i.e., in meditation, visualization, imagination, etc. In our present state of development we can't live without dreams. They're the food of our lives, where the past, present, and future, seemingly in an illogical sequence, can all be projected in a single flash. We first acquaint ourselves with past lives through dreams. The memory of the projection may not be clear. But we can vivify the past life experience and bring it into focus as we begin to interpret it.

I remember a recurring dream about a gloomy, neglected farmhouse, where I lived with three daughters. We all spoke French in the dream, and I wore a long, dark, shapeless skirt. Nothing much would happen; it was simply a brief vignette in which there was a desolate, ominous feeling that the children and I had been left behind. Some years later, traveling through France by car, I saw a house from a distance that was at once familiar to me. We stopped the car, I got out, and a chill came over me. I knew this house.

As I walked around the outside, a woman appeared at the door and asked what she could do for me. In my broken French, I asked if she would be gracious enough to show me her house. I made the excuse that I was interested in this type of architecture. She showed me in and soon was following me as I moved from room to room, knowing my way around perfectly. Every room, every cupboard, every nook and cranny of that house was familiar. Though it was a hot summer day I left shivering, transported into a frightening memory.

Some time later, I visited a psychic. One of the first things she said was that I had had an incarnation in France in which I had three daughters. We were abandoned by the man of the house and our circumstances were so miserable and my condition so despondent that I did away with our lives.

The tragic karma I had incurred in that lifetime in rural France had continued to hang over me, carrying its effect into my present life. Having seen the house, having heard the psychic, the dream ceased to come to me, for I now recognized my duty as a mother, my responsibility to myself and my daughters. I understood what the dream had been saying to me, that life is to be revered against all odds. And now I was done with it. This is an excellent example of material that comes through in dream form which is actually the memory of a past life.

We're continually in the past-present-future in dreaming. We freely roam the cosmos, where everything exists simultaneously in timelessness.

KINDS OF DREAMS

Every dreamer dreams on the level of his or her consciousness; and what is ordinary to one may be fantastic to another. The material each of us receives in dreams depends on our ability to handle it. In any aspect of life we are not given anything we are not ready for. But since people usually do not deal with the symbology of their dreams, they automatically think that what they project is either commonplace, preposterous, out-of-context, or unrelated. The symbols of a dream are most often based on your most recent impressions from a day or two before, but they may have absolutely nothing to do with the content, the message of the dream.

There are precognitive dreams, in which we are able to

glimpse the future. In such dreams, the things you experience will be totally unfamiliar to you; whereas if you dream of a past life the details—though they may be strange—will be more or less familiar to you. With this criteria, you can place the dream in its proper grouping.

A precognitive dream is usually very, very dramatic. If you dream of impending disaster, for example, it's often a prediction about the world in general, not necessarily the dreamer's life. There are people who are in such receivership that precognitive material comes through pertaining to world events: These incidents are highly charged with heavy drama. This is more than a dream, it is a vision. There are other people who receive tragedies or disasters in their dreams concerning their families. During the war, women would often dream about their soldier husbands being injured or killed at the exact second it actually happened. Days or even weeks later, they would receive a telegram of notification. Such dreams are of a precognitive nature, giving us visual access beyond time into events that later come to play themselves out.

The more common form of precognitive dream is something positive in the dreamer's life: a revelation, a mission, something they are going to perform in life. These dreams have to do with the dreamer personally as opposed to the world in general. This type of dream shows you the route—opening a door, going to a window. It answers a riddle and tells you what you can do to resolve a dilemma. A symbol is presented—a key (keys open doors), or an escape hole—that tells you you can get out of a particular situation threatening you within a dream.

When, in the dream state, the urgency is felt to do something—rescue, help, accomplish—but you're lethargic and moving in slow motion, you can't act in time, you can't yell for help, and you're unable to free yourself, you probably are reviewing a past incarnation. The inactivity of the dreamer is the clue that the material projected actually took place in another lifetime. When you are more a spectator than a participant, when you're passive and lying low while the action takes place, or when weird, eerie things are happening around you and you watch it all from some hidden corner and nobody knows you're there, you are clued in that it's your past life you're dealing with.

This kind of a dream reviews things the way they were, not as present-day incidents. These are factual accounts of events that once took place, and the manner in which the drama unfolded. They are repeated the way they happened, and this is the clue that they represent a past incarnation. If a dream pertains to a present situation, it would contain symbols of roads, fields, doors, because there are still many different ways open to you to handle your affairs. But you definitely would get an inkling that something regarding your life today needs different handling, a new point of view, or a fresh approach. Be aware, however, that reviewing a past life has a direct connection with your life today. There are things you didn't resolve then that you need to do now to balance your life.

Whatever occurs or whoever appears in your dreams is a reflection of yourself. There will be people in your dreams that you know and people in your dreams that you do not know in this lifetime. The setting and clothing clue you as to whether you are dreaming about a past incarnation, or having a precognitive dream of people yet to be encountered in your present life. If you're dreaming about a living person whom you know but the setting belongs to another period in time, the dream is likely to be a clue about a relationship in a past incarnation. If you're dreaming about someone you've never met in this lifetime, yet cars, airplanes or other up-to-date details figure in, you might expect to meet such a person in the future. Most likely you have known this person in a previous lifetime.

Often we are confused when a person known to us appears as someone else. "It was my father, but it wasn't really my father." Or "It was a woman I know, but she was a man; but I know it was her." This is a common type of dream that reveals the reincarnation cycles. We pass through both genders again and again, and this feeling, this knowledge of previous lives is clearly available to us in the timelessness of dreams. Sensing within your dreams is all-important, even beyond the meanings of every symbol.

Symbology in dreams frequently predates recorded history. Material we can't immediately identify is flashed in a picture encompassing an entire incarnation from eons ago. The feelings that accompany or follow such dreams are what is important. They are elaborations on the visual flash and are integral to the total meaning of the dream experience. Another factor is your feeling upon awakening from a dream. If you are overcome with guilt or fear, or on the other hand, if you awaken feeling great joy or renewal, totally refreshed, whatever the feelings, they provide the insight into the meaning of your dream content.

A recurring dream is an urgent message that you have not resolved a given problem confronting you, a lesson that will come at you time and time again, until you have understood and taken action. Dreams of guilt will recur over and over, until you face up to and resolve whatever is out of step in your life.

Most important, whether the symbols or stories be past, present, or future, your dreams talk directly to you and pertain to your life right now.

THE SYMBOLOGY OF DREAMS

As a child, I was intrigued by the many dreams I remembered so vividly. And I was curious: I knew intuitively that they pertained to me. They talked to me. They were about me. And I always wanted to find out more.

In my very first year of school, we were taught stories from the Bible, in simplified form for children. And I remember being fascinated with dream interpretation. We were reading about Joseph and his brothers. He had been taken to Egypt, and there he saved his soul through the interpretation of dreams.

Today we're not well-versed in dream interpretation. The value of dreams escapes us. We owe it to ourselves to become acquainted with the dream language because the symbologies are just as meaningful to our waking experiences as to our dream-life. The message is the same whether you're in your conscious or your subconscious state. You can learn to interpret your dreams by intelligently observing the nature of the material that appears. Whatever the symbol—animal, object, or person—first examine its inherent quality and function: *"What does the symbol DO?"* Then consider your *attitude* toward it and its function, *because symbols mean different things to different people.*

A dog to one person can be lovable, for example, and to someone else frightening. Let's say you love dogs. Dogs by nature are loyal and obedient to their master. Therefore, it would be your loyalty to yourself we'd be dealing with if you dreamt about a dog. Loyalty is also protection: no matter where you are, you're safe. So a dog in a dream implies security, protection, and devotion—*if* you love dogs. On the other hand, if you dislike dogs, then the symbology addresses itself to cowardice, insecurity, and fear of new situations.

The same premise applies to cats. Some people are horrified of cats, because of their sudden movements. If they dreamt about a cat, it would have an entirely different meaning than it would have for someone who adores and lives with felines. No matter how one feels about cats in general, loyalty would not enter into it, because cats are such independent creatures by nature.

In other words, you always have to take into consideration the animal you dream about, its natural environment and inherent qualities: how it performs, lives, eats, and behaves. You have to consider that first; and then your relationship to it. We may dream about animals that are extinct.

We no longer have a conscious memory of them. Or we may dream of unfamiliar machines, airships, or spiritual powers and abilities that seem extraordinary. These are things that were and are and indicate an innovative mind at work.

Dreaming about animals, however, is indicative of our planet Earth experience. Perhaps we are a bit too earthy, too physical—depending on the animal projected. If you dream about lizards or alligators, your consciousness is reminded of its lowliness, its earthy, physical aspect (such animals living in the mud and mire). A dream of this nature urges you to raise your level. Whereas if you dream about a bird in flight, it naturally indicates a greater loftiness of ideas and expression within your consciousness.

Most of your dreams are in a direct conversational form and a message to you. These dreams usually contain symbols familiar to us all—parts of the body, a car, ship, house, things representing the dreamer directly. To interpret the symbol of a bedroom, for example, think in terms of what takes place there—secret possibilities, hidden things, or sexual connotations. Basically, the bedroom deals with privacy, secrecy, intimacy, and rest. Also consider if the dreamer is an adult or a child (or a chambermaid, for that matter).

If a dream takes place in a kitchen, you know it is concerned with food, nourishment, and indulgence for the physical body. You need to break the dream down into each part and its function so that you can better translate the symbols. Then you can understand how it applies to you. A house in a dream usually has three levels: upper, middle, and basement. They are all levels of the dreamer. The basement is your subconscious mind, your storage house. The middle level is your conscious mind, your daily thinking activity. And upstairs deals with your higher self, your aspirations. The house is you. Is the foundation sound? Are you together? Is the house shaky? Do you need to work on yourself? If you dream about numbers, you would want to know a little bit about numerology in order to understand what they are saying to you. Each number has its own vibration.

Many times within a dream, there's a sense of someone being with you, or walking with you, but you do not have a specific image of that person. You simply feel that he or she is close. Possibly without a face or a body you sense this presence. Yet you know, through your sensing, whether they're on your right or on your left. The symbology here is very definite: on your right they represent the higher you, your aspirations, your potential, and your right path in life; on your left, they represent the more earthbound you, your fears, your old habits, and a wrong direction. The reverse may be true for people who are left-handed; since they lead with their left, this may be their positive direction. Again, the context is very important: If you're dreaming about a road in England, for example (where the left side of the road is used, then left is the positive direction, whether you're left-handed or not. Something occurring on a left-handed person's left *can* be her positive direction; but it also involves right or wrong *within* herself.

Going up a hill in a dream means you're ascending; going down, descending—spiritually, consciousness-wise. If you come to a crossroads and you don't know which way to go, well, that speaks for itself.

If you dream about crystal clear water, it's a dream of the clarity of creative things to come. If the water is cloudy or muddy, then the dreamer is in a great state of confusion.

If you dream about fire, the symbol is purification. Again, it depends on the context and the dreamer. In a fireplace fire can be something beautiful; if the house is burning down, it is destructive. So what takes place within the dream in association with fire determines whether the content is progressive or destructive. The person's attitude toward fire is also important.

One of the most common experiences in a dream is that someone is chasing you. This is clearly an indication that you are guilt-ridden and running away from responsibility and your problems. Someone coming at you with a weapon also indicates guilt. We at all times act as judge and jury, meting out our own punishment which is acted out and represented through other people in the dream reality. This is demonstrated in dreams in just the same way it is in our conscious living. In dream form, if you have committed a wrong, you immediately enact your own punishment and someone invariably comes after you with gun, rope, knife, or whatever.

Oftentimes, it could be an actual experience from a past life, retribution meted out under the karmic law of cause-and-effect. The process of self-judgment is constantly at work, whether the dream deals with your present actions or those of a previous life. All of our experiences serve a purpose, but our dreams are especially aimed at our consciousness as we go through this life.

Many people dream about losing things: their purse or wallets, their valuables. These items directly indicate a loss of consciousness, which truly ought to be our most prized possession. When consciousness is slipping, we're not working on ourselves. So if you dream about losing a wallet or keys, the dream is meant to remind you that you need to set forth greater effort in accord with your potential.

People frequently dream about being lost in a strange country, they don't know how to find their way back. Again, this is an indication of their level of consciousness dropping, losing their bearings and grip on life. Others will dream of being in foreign countries, where they are versed in the language and perfectly at home. These are dreams of actual past incarnations. The former may also be, but in that past life you did not sufficiently work on your consciousness or your spiritual unfoldment. Therefore, you are still meeting it in this life, where it alerts you to work harder on raising your consciousness. You are still lost, and that's the message, the reminder to do something about it now.

If you dream about a candle being lit, the flame is giving

you light and direction. A white candle denotes purification. You may be on holy ground. Even the flickering of the candle has significance: if it burns well and high, if the flame is steady, or if it is struggling and always on the brink of going out, the symbolism is self-explanatory.

Write down your dream. Two days later review it intelligently. The message will reveal itself. You have to reduce every object, every thing, every person to its natural function and inherent quality and then relate them to yourself. If you dream about someone, you have to recognize his characteristics. Is he sinister? Is he beautiful? *It's your dream, so everything in it applies directly to you.*

Beautiful music? Harmony, love, and peace. Shrill, discordant tones? Disharmony, resentment, and anger. The same applies to colors and composition in paintings. Anything dealing with the arts in dreams concerns the dreamer's creativity and spirituality.

Often a dream of first love denotes that a new love is on the horizon.

If you dream about flowers and lush fields and exquisite colors, your road in life is unlimited. There is nothing you can't do, nothing you can't undertake. The path is wide open to you.

Red is vitality, energy, and love, but it can also be anger (seeing red, getting red in the face). Again, it would depend on other symbols within the dream.

White is purity, or it could be atrophy. If you dream about being in the middle of nowhere and everything is covered with snow, it would certainly not symbolize purity, but rather a frozen condition in your own development. Whereas a white flower would denote a ceremony, such as a wedding, or a birth of a child.

My daughter Luana recently had a dream about a girlfriend wearing a green dress. Green symbolizes envy. She realized that there must be some jealousy in her, though not necessarily about this particular girl.

Blue is a healing color. People who are sick often dream in blue, which indicates a healing process is taking place. Blue comes to tell them that they are going to recover. When one is past recovery, the dreams will take on shades of gray and black. Black is certainly the most negative side projecting itself. It stands for death, sickness, violence, and lies. A dark room has sinister overtones in a dream.

Pale yellow is social activity, but in a flippant context, as befits a gossip or busybody. Yellow is a snobbish, aristocratic color; it is also the color of spring and regeneration. In the Mayan civilization, yellow was the color used in association with death. Perhaps rather than focusing on death, they took it a step further to represent new life, knowing that with each death comes a new beginning. Gold is a highly spiritual color, as in the golden aura or halo.

A car, house, ship, or road symbolize your person. If the car is broken down, your health might be slipping. Still you should not, overlook having the car checked because it may need mechanical attention. But more often than not, the car is you, the dreamer, not the actual vehicle.

A road is definitely your path in life. Is it open and wide? Obstructed? Bumpy?

A ship's anchor? Your steadfastness. In whole or in part, the symbol characterizes you.

Dreams about flying have different connotations. Children often dream about flying, and to them it is an actual experience because they are in the act of catching the soul as it re-enters the body. You must always consider who the dreamer is: child, adult, man, or woman. A pilot dreaming about flying a plane would convey an entirely different meaning since flying is his normal activity. For the average person, planes and flying represent freedom, soaring aspirations, and new ideas.

Dreams about clothing: a hat, you're dealing with ideas, because it goes on your head; shoes or socks, you're dealing with understanding because they go on your feet and what kind of a foothold do you have on this planet Earth? Color, too, is important. If the hat is red, perhaps your thoughts are angry. A white hat may have to do with a new idea. Clothing covers certain parts of the body. Consider what that part performs and this is where the symbology originates—from parts of the body, not the actual garment. Yet it all comes into play. Dream about a shirt without sleeves, or one in tatters, in all probability your faith (which is your arms) isn't working.

Often people find themselves nude in their dreams. This type of dream usually occurs after the person has caused embarrassment to someone else. They now have to stand naked in order to feel their own embarrassment. Others can dream about being nude and not feel ashamed at all. For them nudity represents relaxation and freedom.

Dreaming about teeth, or losing them, means that in daily life you talked unkindly about other people. The dream comes to remind you that corrections in your behavior patterns are necessary. Unusually large teeth in a dream would indicate that you've exaggerated and magnified the truth out of all proportion in recent, everyday life. Tiny teeth mean you're mincing words and not expressing yourself.

When you dream about different parts of the body it is important how they appear. You have to associate the symbols with their condition. Hands, for instance, are giving. Were the hands in your dream swollen? Bony? Hanging loosely? In that way you can understand the symbology more closely.

We constantly reveal ourselves. As a matter of fact, we beg to reveal ourselves not only to others but, more importantly, to ourselves. Our dreams constantly gnaw at us and speak to us directly. Every role that is played out by another in your dream is an aspect of you, the dreamer, including the villain who may appear to chase or harass you. Everyone we encounter in our waking hours or in our dreams, everyone that we admonish or criticize, simply mirrors an aspect of ourselves. For if we did not contain the very thing we dislike, we could not see it in another, just as the good, beautiful, loving, and harmonizing factors encountered in our lives also reflect an aspect of ourselves.

You need to interpret all of your dreams as useful, intelligent, and most of all, *applicable to yourself.* Then they will make sense in what they say to you, in the way they talk to you.

Self-revelation in dreams is only constructive if we work with it. This direct guidance comes to show us our higher beings and what we must eliminate in order to build new patterns for ourselves and a more purposeful life.

Sleep as an Escape

Often we feel a great need to find out something more about ourselves. By deliberately going into a sleep state, we prepare ourselves for insight through our dream material. Perhaps, we say, not quite understanding why, "I'm tired. I need a nap. I must get away from it all." In effect, what we're saying is that we need ten minutes of replenishment, a different source of nourishment to sustain ourselves in the waking state. Unconsciously we know we are going to receive sustenance from our nap. It will give us the energy to cope with the outer reality.

Waking from sleep is the same in reverse. When you can't take any more of the dream-reality, you awaken in order to refresh yourself.

Many people sleep too much. They want to disconnect themselves, through sleep, from their daily activity. If the periods of sleep become too long, the conscious mind will sever itself from the subconscious mind. Too much sleep will deaden all realities.

There is also excess wakefulness, the other extreme, where one is afraid to go to sleep, to make contact with the dream-reality. A lot of people cannot sleep at all. They're afraid because they don't wish to deal with the content of their dreams, whether they remember the dream or not.

Too much of anything—food, drugs, sex, sleep, whatever—and we cut ourselves off, we deaden ourselves. We exist within a continuum in which we find our balance. This principle applies in every area of our lives. If you stay awake too long, you will lose your equilibrium. Sleep and dreaming connect us, giving us continuity. If you reduce the hours, the span between the poles of sleep and waking, you can better connect your subconscious and conscious minds into one continuously flowing totality.

You'll find that if you sleep less (catnap, so to speak), your continuity is more present. You're more together. Whereas if you've slept around the clock, you wake up feeling numb and totally disconnected from any reality.

You want to continually reconnect yourself with whatever is taking place within these seemingly separate realities. Usually, the conscious, subconscious, and superconscious minds are operating on their own. You experience total immersion here, total immersion there without realizing that everything is happening at once. It's all happening now, simultaneously. Seeing it in this limitless way, the past, present and future become one. Time dissolves.

THE INFINITE CONTINUITY

We could not exist without the vast material that goes on in dream form. The seeming reality that we identify with would render us insane if we didn't experience in dreams the *true* reality, the fulfillment of our inner beings.

The moment you enter your dream world, you pick up its continuity and reality. You fall asleep and immediately feel at home, sensing its flow. Just as when you awaken, you pick up the reality of your daily activity where you left off the day before. And you are at home within that continuity as well. The same sense of continuity links us to our past lives. Having lived before, the memory of your past life carries on and forms a bridge with this present life.

It's all one continual process.

All of these states make up the sum total of what you are, every instant of your being. You carry this aggregate with you at all times, all realities at once—whether awake, dreaming, in the spirit-world or in an incarnation. It all comes to comprise one huge continuum. Each reality is not something unto itself, separate. It is an important aspect of your wholeness. Whatever the reality, you must connect one to the other.

You can catch, you can feel, you can sense this continuity better with brief intervals between sleep and waking. You will see the interweaving that takes place between the different realities. In this way you can tie them together for yourself. This is a key to mastering your destiny.

If the total mind—conscious, subconscious, and superconscious—were completely unified, there would be no need to dream at all. All your realities would merge into one. You would then be living all realities at once. At that point, you would have solved all your riddles and become one with God. You would be a realized being, free will would be truly yours to exercise for the first time.

When you're integrated and have grasped all your realities, nothing but expression remains, yet you still have a choice: Do you wish to express in this form of life or in another? On the earth plane or elsewhere in the cosmos? Understanding this, having mastered your destiny, you become extremely selective.

By unifying all realities, our potential is fantastic. Nothing is beyond possibility. The only reason anything is impossible to an individual mind is because that mind is not connected with its total continuity. We tend to look for specific, finite answers. The laws of the universe do not operate that way. We need to enter the realm of infinity where everything connects and where everything can talk to us.

CHAPTER SIX

IT'S THE BEST THING THAT EVER HAPPENED TO YOU

Anyone who has ever made a contribution to life has always been a person who confronted adversity with an optimistic and positive mind.

AN ATTEMPTED SUICIDE

A reading was given to a woman during which it was indicated that her daughter showed suicidal tendencies. It was further revealed that the subject would have to reach out to communicate with her troubled child, lest there be grave consequences. Soon afterward, the daughter swallowed a bottle of sleeping pills, but was fortunately saved when the doctors pumped her stomach.

The woman later told me that the reading had prepared her for this possibility. But instead of handling it right away, as she might have, before her daughter did something drastic, she procrastinated. Apparently she needed the shock of the experience to mobilize her energies. Only after the suicide attempt did she really begin to make contact with her daughter. This necessitated the woman subordinating her own ego, almost disregarding herself, in order to bring another closer.

We deal with things in life only when we're truly ready. Could the woman I speak of have dealt with the problem before her girl took the pills, I'm sure she would have. As it turned out, she received an intimation about her daughter which alerted her to the situation and more or less prepared the way for a later reconciliation. She was not quite ready to take action before the suicide attempt but, subsequently, their relationship has flowered and become quite beautiful. The mother has begun to see her daughter as an individual and no longer centers her thoughts solely on herself. Sometimes we need such drastic events to awaken us. Today this woman sees that it was the best thing that has ever happened to her.

YOU ATTRACT WHAT YOU ARE

Everything we experience, every encounter, every exchange in our lives, talks to us. To the individual who perceives life with feeling and sensitivity, everything has specific meaning. Whatever you encounter in your life (even an animal on the street) pertains to you and directly involves you. You must make this connection. Habitually, we regard the world as something outside us. But there are enormous benefits to be gained from equating everything with the self, from seeing our reflection in any given situation, person, or thing for that matter. This is the material we must work with: the good, the bad, the obvious, and the subtle.

In dream form, everything and anything represents the dreamer. Every aspect is in us. The same holds true in our waking life. Everything is a representation of you, whether you see it or not. Once you equate this way, you have an incredible amount to gain from each experience. Observe your attitude to whatever is going on around you. Once you do, then the experience will directly talk to you.

Since everything you encounter is an aspect of yourself, your tolerance will begin to grow toward things you were once quick to judge and denounce. You're ready to make changes. If you deem something unfavorable in someone else, you've made a judgment that merely reflects yourself. Set it as an example. Promise yourself that in a future, similar situation you will not be judgmental, critical, or prejudiced. What you don't like in others mirrors something in you. Viewed like this, you can change your attitudes to something more wholesome and more beautiful. Everything is always dependent on your relationship and attitude to the experience. What is your reaction as you meet it? How does it talk to you? How do you feel about it? Whether things, people, events seem meaningful or superficial—they are all you! This is what you have to examine.

A woman came for a reading, upset because a man she worked with and cared for did not reciprocate her love. She blamed it all on another woman in her office. "Since that woman came to work, nothing has been the same." She was full of accusations. It was all her fault; if the other woman hadn't been there, this never would have happened. She went through a box of tissues, talking and sobbing. It was very painful to her.

Never for a moment did she consider her part in this situation. She could not see her own involvement—what she herself had done to cause and in effect bring this other woman into the picture. The other woman really had nothing to do with it. Rather, it was her own constant demands and criticism of the man that created the rival.

We have nothing to gain by blaming others and excusing ourselves. Conversely, we have everything to gain when we reflect on any given situation or problem through our own equation in reference to ourselves. The atmosphere you walk in creates your reality. You are responsible for the world in which you find yourself. Too often we make other persons the target, naming them the culprit. Before we realize it, we have set a whole chain reaction in motion and our negativity calls forth negative responses. Then we find ourselves looking for more material to get upset about; it becomes a false release from the accumulated pressure.

When you're caught in such a vicious cycle, you're totally out of step with life. Your negative self continues to conjure up material that can only lead to further self-rejection. The ego-self reviews and focuses on everything from a material point of view only. The soul is completely squashed and can find no expression whatsoever. The outer world becomes all-important, as though it were the only reality of your existence. Once this transference of priorities to the external world takes place, you are caught in a web of false values. You are lost.

Realized beings we are not. If we were, we wouldn't be here on this planet Earth. We must learn from each experience and our lesson begins when we stop judging, condemning, and hating ourselves. Then we start to realize that each experience is never an end in itself but only a new beginning.

Sometimes progress may seem slow. Observe yourself during periods of negativity. See how quickly things go wrong. It makes you wonder to see the universal law work so fast. In negativity we are charged with enormous energy. Wrong experiences come into devastating fulfillment immediately. By and large, when we are in a positive frame of mind, we are not so charged. We're in a much lower key, much more subdued, and we do not get results as quickly. But work at it, develop the inner resources, and you can gain equal power for the positive.

Observe negative, ego-based, selfish persons. They have incredible energy and can tear down in a flash what it took a lifetime to build. We are brought up to think negatively. Changing to a more positive, attitude must necessarily involve uncertainty. Learning a new lesson is not easy. We're treading unfamiliar ground.

An accident, illness, argument—all these are the immediate results of a negative charge. But where are the immediate results of your positive energies? They will become more apparent as you practice and keep at it. The more diligent the efforts the quicker you develop into a powerhouse that will bring about right results in your life.

We don't realize how we slowly commit suicide daily through self-pity, self-doubt, and self-indulgence. All are foreign to the soul and this is where the conflict occurs: the soul versus the ego-self. The ego-self, which is negative, is a projection based on a false premise, and the soul, which is positive and always in an objective state, shrinks away from the ego-self. The soul has its own expression that knows nothing about materialism. When the ego-self projects, the soul gets out of the way and lies dormant. The ego-self takes over and goes on a rampage of destructiveness. When finally exhausted, it seeks out the soul all over again. That is our true sustenance, without which life has no purpose and we are nothing.

The soul knows everything, but when the ego-self takes over, the soul wants nothing to do with it. The soul disassociates from the ego-self and then we cannot cope. Calamity stares us straight in the face. The negative force takes over and turns us into a demon. Not that a demon enters the soul; rather, the intellect, the ego-self, introduces demonic forces that leave nothing for the soul to feed on.

When the soul is suppressed, we must pay the penalty and the first thing to go is the physical body. Ultimately, if the soul cannot express itself through the physical body, then it will find some other mode, some other form. It gives up the body. Obviously this vessel is not providing the fertile ground for the soul. The soul slowly departs and the body deteriorates. What happens to the soul? It reenters the spirit world for fortification and prepares itself for experience elsewhere, possibly in another body and in another incarnation.

The soul is always ready and willing to be recognized. It never dies. It never gives up. The soul has always been and always will be. It *is*, at all times. When you're ready, your soul is there, waiting. Once you can make contact you can be in step with everything in life. But if you don't treasure your soul and maintain an intimate relationship with it, you will pave a road of difficulty and hardship for yourself.

Whatever is satisfying, purposeful, joyful, loving in your expression of yourself is born of the soul. The more joy, love, and beauty we express, the more nourishment we provide for the soul.

Everything we program ourselves for we're going to attract. The soul knows only abundance, while the ego-self identifies with lack. Every time you set yourself a budget based in negative thinking, for instance, you attract lack into your life. If you say, "I have to put two dollars aside for this problem that might come and a dollar for that one that might come," you take a step closer to materializing the feared situation. When you say, "I can't afford this and I can't afford that," then you're telling your subconscious mind *you can't afford it.* Subconscious mind then makes sure of it. A plan of lack will produce lack in the actual experience. And a plan of plenty will produce an experience of plenty, materially or otherwise. You have to use your common sense, of course, and live within resources actually at your disposal; but if you preoccupy yourself with thoughts of the rainy day you have to save for, then it's certainly going to pour.

When I began studying with Dr. Barker, I had a great deal of enthusiasm. I was so caught up with his concepts, I found myself wishing something would happen so that I could find out how I would react, how I would work with it. I just couldn't wait: I thought I would know how to handle anything. One day I was driving along a newly completed highway and I heard a thumping sound. I came to a stop and discovered my car had a flat tire. At that moment, I found myself wishing I had paid more attention to my husband the many times he had explained to me how to change a tire. I stood there wondering how I was going to get out of this predicament. Since it was a new road, there was virtually no traffic going in either direction. I began to feel I would be stranded forever.

Suddenly I remembered Barker's precepts and I said to myself, "Oh, ye of little faith. Here's a test, and already you're falling apart." With that, I calmed myself. I surrendered to the higher intelligence and knew everything would be all right. I simply envisioned my car in perfect working operation and me on my way.

Seemingly out of nowhere came a single car. It crossed the lanes and headed directly toward me as I stood next to my vehicle. A man got out and proceeded to take full charge. First, he moved my car off the road. Then he changed the tire. I said to him, "You know, God sent you to me." I learned he was a mechanic, yet he refused to accept money for his work. Nor would he give me his name or address so I could send him a gift for his kindness. He drove away, leaving me to reflect on the fact that everything is always just as it should be. If you have the conviction of your beliefs, the appropriate channel will always open up for you and answer your immediate needs. This is truly the power of the soul.

TURN IT AROUND

To experience life to the full, greet *everything* that happens to you with an accepting heart because it's the best thing that ever happened to you. Inevitably, everything you experience is for your own good, a lesson to further your development.

When my husband left, I said to myself, "Grace, it's happening to you, not to somebody else. Therefore you are the responsible party. It won't help to conjure up in your mind the rights and wrongs, the who did what to whom. None of that is going to help. The point is that since you're in it you have attracted it. So now pick yourself up and know that it's the best thing that ever happened to you. Rise above it!"

When something happens over which you no longer have any control, you must see it as the best thing that ever happened to you. It immediately signifies a new road will open up for you. You have to assume that; you have to take it from a constructive premise. This necessitates letting go, freeing yourself from recriminations, justifications, and hurts. It's the hurts, wounds, and guilt that are the killers that we nourish and get stuck on. They obscure our view of the new possibilities and opportunities facing us. By declaring, "It's the best thing that ever happened," and believing it, you begin to let go of past wrongs and are now motivated in a new direction. You have turned the situation to your advantage. Soon you will know for a fact that it's the best thing that ever happened to you.

Take everything that happens to you as a new foundation for something good in your life. When you think this way, something larger takes over, attracted by the nucleus of positive energy emanating from you. Suddenly you can see the waste, the stupidity, and above all, what it did to you. Once you see it with utmost clarity, you can discard it all and can now move on.

We are reminded daily of what we could do better. You may wake up, for example, grouchy and out-of-sorts—never mind what caused it. Immediately, write a note to yourself go to the positive. List all the good things in your life. Surely you will find something. In this way the energy is moved in the right direction.

I woke up moody the other day. The way I talked to the children was snappy and thoughtless, and they responded in like manner. When I realized what was going on, I stopped what I was doing and went into the kitchen where I have a little blackboard on which I write messages to myself. First I started with "I am." "I am" makes me sit up and take note of myself. "I am"—I perk up, I open my ears, I turn on a switch. That day I wrote "I am happy. My children are the greatest. I am blessed." I returned with a completely different attitude, and the girls responded immediately with their own positive feelings. The difference was like day and night.

These are the little things that, practiced daily, bring back your awareness. Nothing is too trivial, for it sets up your whole atmosphere and if you allow the negative to continue, your day will go from bad to worse.

Another thing: I never go to bed upset, no matter what happened in the course of the day. Nor would I allow the children to. I may have had sharp moments, but I don't dwell on them. Before bedtime, I always make it my business to be sure that the girls and I retire with a good feeling about ourselves. In this way, we wake up the next day refreshed. It's not only healthy for them but healthy for me as well. Try it. It might work for you, too.

GIVING IN

I used to have trouble with cars. They had never been a problem until my husband left. Of course I'm aware that a car is a direct representation of yourself—it's your own mind. (Most dream symbols are representational in your daily life as well.) I'd go out, and my car wouldn't start. No matter how many times I would say to myself, "You're not meant to leave today, you're not meant to go anyplace," I still knew enough to realize that that car wasn't starting because my thinking was off. My mind affected the vehicle and the inanimate object performed accordingly. An hour later I would come out, in an entirely different frame of mind, and lo and behold, it would kick over the first time around.

When the car wouldn't start, I also took it to mean that perhaps I wasn't meant to go to a given place. Who knows what disaster was averted when I was prevented from driving in an angry, confused state? All these things should talk to us, in the sense that we don't want to force anything. It's always good to give in to things, to yield and accept. Never resist a situation that you can't do anything about. Your resistance cuts off the natural flow of events. Once you accept things as they are, the flow continues.

Especially within the context of an argument, instead of engaging in it, try saying, "You're absolutely right" in an honest tone of voice. That should stop the battle. The other party can't make war alone. Once the atmosphere becomes receptive you can make whatever point you wish. Allow the other person to express his view. Introduce a new atmosphere. You will find your adversary has forgotten what he was arguing about. Now you can relate to one another.

The same thing applies within the flow of life. Whatever comes into your sphere, your immediate acceptance of it is all-important. By dropping your resistance and facing the facts as they are, you become dignified. This is an integral part of giving and receiving. When we examine ourselves, we tend to be self-condemning, when we should be self-approving. Not in false pride, but in true dignity.

Give people ground, give them breathing space, and give them time. This is what I do when people come to me for readings. At first I let them say whatever presses on them. I have plenty of time to introduce a new thought. If I introduce one too soon, they're so tuned in to their problems that they can't hear me. They're not receptive. Their whole routine has been too well rehearsed. Eventually there comes a point when they've spilled it all; they're empty, spent. They let go. And that is when they can take in a new thought, when there's room for exchanging fresh ideas.

A Different Kind of Death

A great deal of work is being done with people who are dying, using certain drugs and other means to help them face their death. Certainly this is good. More challenging perhaps than helping people through a passage from this world into the next would be to apply these same energies to help them see their true condition and involvement with life. If people can be taught to alleviate their fear of dying, they can with greater intensity remove their fear of living—and realize the unimportance of dying!

Dying is the best thing that could happen to us. Not the death most people are so concerned with, the kind that puts you six feet under, the death of the physical person. Rather, in terms of life, we actually need to die to many things. We need to die to old patterns, negativity, worries, and destructive habits. With each death you discover a new beginning, a new you.

Most of us are enslaved by old habits, performing our tasks from patterns no longer relevant to our lives, making us automatons most of the time because rarely do we bother with a new thought or idea. How much selective, deliberate thinking do we actually do? Usually very little. It's all done for us. Without realizing it, we are slaves to habit and public opinion. Try breaking a habit, be it ever so small. You can see yourself anew in trying to do away with an old pattern. To break a habit—without replacing it with another—is a wonderful experience. In the process, you will make an exciting discovery about yourself.

We come into this Earth experience with a great deal of reverence. Therefore, the body has to be regarded as a temple. It is the house of your soul on this planet, the outer expression. As such, you don't want to—indeed you can't afford to—abuse that which houses your greatest treasure. Take good care of your body, and remember, anything done to excess, in any of the five senses, defiles it.

This applies to any excess or indulgence—sex, food, drink, smoking, whatever. By becoming hooked to outer stimuli and sensation, you dull your senses. More importantly, when your soul moves into the spirit-world, it will have tremendous difficulty adjusting to its surroundings. Addicted to earthly habits, unable to detach yourself from the longing for them, you will suffer terribly before you finally adjust to the spirit-world atmosphere. It is literally like a drug addict going through withdrawal.

Children usually have great resistance to change. They have just gone through an important and difficult transformation by coming into this world. They haven't gotten their bearings as yet. The possibility of changes occurring here is frightening to them. Yet they adjust quickly, because in their essence-state of being they have selected this Earth experience, necessitating a program of change, and the memory of this selection is still fresh in their subconscious minds. Notice, however, that some infants do have a very difficult time adjusting, based on the same phenomenon of habit-forming enslavery—whether it be in the spirit-world or here on Earth. This is all related to past lives: habits formed here; habits formed there. Coming to Earth, not adjusting; going into the spirit-world, not adjusting. For some people it takes twenty years or more just to get their bearings. They cannot orientate themselves in the spirit-world nor can they organize their stay upon this Earth. It can take years just to know where they are, let alone who they are.

In this lifetime we need to shed our futile devotion to old habits and pay less attention to the trivia of the senses. We have the opportunity to free ourselves from these obsessions if we see them in the right way. Look at a cigarette, for example, and observe what fascinates you, what holds you chained to it. You have allowed a pattern to develop, giving a silly weed power over you. See it for what it is and you will say, "How ridiculous that this weed should have so much power over my life that I can't do without it!" In that moment of realization, you may well be ready to throw it away. After all, who's the master, the cigarette or you?

These are little exercises we have to do all the time. That's what we're doing here on Earth. We're testing ideas. All our experiences are for our own gain, unfoldment, and growth. We must learn from them and move on.

Awareness has to come from within; but we should not neglect the outer domain—this temple, our body. A lot more caring should enter into our thinking and behavior concerning our bodies, because we indeed represent a higher intelligence. If you slouch, become depressed, moody, or self-pitying, ask yourself, "Is this the way I would represent a higher intelligence? Is this a valid representation of God? Or is it instead my own little ego at work, my negativity, my conjuring, indeed my own creation?"

Meditate about life. Consider all the magnificence around you. You will see that anything that you find wrong in your life is of your own making. God certainly does not single you out as if to say, "Look, there you are! Let's give you something rotten today!" God is impersonal. To make the power from within work for us, we must first personalize God. That can only be done by living an ideal, affirmative life. Anything else cannot be Godlike. If you have any concept of God at all, it must be an image of perfection. Imperfection certainly does not relate to God. It is of your own making, the product of your ego, and to that limitation, you must die. You must banish it in order to be rejuvenated, re-energized. You need to die to old habits to have the full sense of life.

The one and only place where the intellect is important is in considering our relationship to God. Don't make excuses for the way you behave. That will never further you, it will only retard your growth. Use your intellect to conceptualize a higher being—what you *can* be, what is *in* you, what you *need* and *want* to exemplify in your daily activity.

BEING RIGHT DOESN'T MATTER

When my mother passed on, I asked my father to come to this country to live with us. Shortly after his arrival, my husband decided to make out a will, and it necessitated that I go with him to his lawyer to cosign the document. Now, I do not believe in insurance and I certainly do not believe in wills. The reason I do not believe in such papers is that they put you under a law of attraction that would eventually deliver tragic experiences into your life. Yet, foolishly, I went along.

Papa said that he would like to go, too. So all of us went to the lawyer, and before I knew it, I had signed on the bottom line. The signing became epidemic and my father impulsively decided to make out his own will. I had no idea what it contained and cared less.

Soon afterward, things became exceedingly difficult at home and as a result Papa was asked to leave by my husband. A few days later my eldest brother called. "What kind of a daughter are you?" he demanded. "What did you do to Papa?" I told him I didn't know what he was talking about. "You forced Papa to make out a will and leave everything to you," he shouted. "You robbed him!"

I was furious. I went to my father's new abode (my brother was there, too), and walked in like a demon. "How dare you?" I screamed at my father. I simply could not fathom his motives. "Whoever asked you to give me anything? What right have you to say that I forced you into signing a will to bequeath me everything? Give it all to your son for all I care. He's waiting for it." My father turned white. I slammed the door and out I went. I wasn't about to wait for a reply.

A week passed, during most of which I sat deep in thought. The atmosphere of ill-feelings between my father and me began to bother me deeply. In my meditation I tossed it about: "What differences does it make if you're right or wrong? Look at the pain you're going through. And look at the pain that you have inflicted on your father; he's hurting, too!"

My father was getting along in years. I said to myself, "I have a chance here to do something to create better feelings. How would I feel if something were to happen to him and we had not resolved our differences? I would end up bearing terrible guilt, because I would have missed a precious opportunity." It bothered me a lot. "Let me take care of this swiftly," I decided. I wanted to initiate a good feeling that would create its own chain reaction in reciprocation. I was determined to resolve all grievances between us.

I went to my father and asked for forgiveness. Had he asked what there was to forgive, I would not have known how to answer. I went and said, "I'm very sorry that I have hurt you. Will you please forget the whole thing like it never happened?" I meant every word. I came to him, not in belligerence, but with an open heart. My father was deeply touched. Unable to speak he reached for a handkerchief and dried his tears.

All I remember (and that's all we'll ever remember about anything—not the time and place, but the emotions that we experience) was a feeling of goodwill. That feeling was paramount in my father and me; it was a sense of love. There was a reciprocal flow between us. It truly didn't matter any longer who was right or wrong. The act of forgiveness always brings about a simple resolve. It gives us an opportunity to show ourselves as the greater beings we truly are.

I had pushed aside my intellectualizing about right and wrong and simply pursued my feelings of love and peace that I knew were so important. It became crucial that these good feelings be expressed. Not how, not right, not wrong, and no judgment of any kind—just a simple gesture of extending good feelings toward another human being.

We usually think ourselves so right under most circumstances that we never dream of saying, "I'm sorry" when we might well be in the wrong. This is where we get stuck— judging right or wrong—evaluating and criticizing. We should always examine our feelings first: "How do I feel about the situation, the person, the object, anything?" This should be our foremost question. Is being "right" worth disharmony within the self? Is being "wrong" worth defending? Examine the pain and anguish. Look at the price we pay for our righteousness.

We need to resolve all the negativities in our lives. And being right is of little significance. I was driving with a friend once, and suddenly another car came straight at us. I pulled off the road to let it by. My friend said, "You know, you shouldn't have done that. You had the right-of-way."

I replied, "What good is it to be right, and be dead?" We need to yield more readily, because life and love are truly precious.

You Can't Escape

If you are to come into your own, you must selectively exclude other people's thoughts and actions. You come to this planet to experiment, to experience, and to grow. You mustn't close the door on life's opportunities. You need to allow them to develop. Most important of all, you have to want to work things out.

If you truly realized that the purpose of your being here is to grow, to perfect, to work things out for yourself, you would *welcome every problem as an opportunity*. Each moment is the greatest challenge, the best thing that ever happened to you. The more difficult the problem, the greater the challenge in working it out. Viewed from that aspect, there isn't a problem challenging enough. By applying your mind, by focusing your attention on the solution, problems dissolve almost immediately, because your thought processes are so creative they automatically produce resolution.

The mistakes we make, the errors we commit, the wrongs we do to others, all these are directed against ourselves. They reflect the breaking of immutable laws. God is love. Love is law. If you break the law (whether higher or earthly) by your inherent need to judge yourself, your innermost being quests for forgiveness. There is a tremendous need for unification within us to right every wrong, correct every mistake. We do this intuitively, through our inner awareness. A feeling deep within truly talks to us. But we must be aware; otherwise, we may reason and rationalize everything away. Excusing ourselves merely increases conflict, delays development, and more dangerously, builds new karma.

We all experience turmoil and frustration. We all have our shortcomings. See these as your opportunities for good, which speed up your unfoldment, because your development is eternally at stake. In this light, you can't help but change your attitude toward yourself and others. Embrace your opportunities. Enlightenment will follow. No matter how noble your thinking, nothing will be accomplished by self-justification. Sooner or later, you will have to confront yourself. So why delay?

The challenges are phenomenal and endless. You can't escape from yourself; you have yourself without end. But you can transcend and know that it's the best thing that ever happened to you.

CHAPTER SEVEN

HEALTH IS OUR HERITAGE

*As long as you believe that the physical body
and not the mind is responsible for your
well- being, you can't affect health.*

HEALTH IS YOUR STATE OF MIND

We can make ourselves sick, and we can make ourselves well. The healing power is in us. Everything begins, is experienced, and ends in the mind. Most of the time we are robotlike. We do little original thinking. Yet we need to be more vigilant, like detectives observing ourselves and life around us.

The body does not think or act by itself. Your health is dependent on your general state of mind, your disposition, and day-to-day flow. Check your average thinking, your overall attitude. Are you a happy, contented person or are you a moody, depressed individual?

The higher intelligence can only create positively. Nothing is ever created from a negative source. It is human thinking, as opposed to higher mind, that introduces negativity. By nature, we are happy, healthy people; yet we are brought up to believe otherwise. We are taught from childhood to identify our ailments and discomforts, and before you know it we are looking for them. When people are sick, they dwell on their sickness, they focus on aches and pains, not realizing that they are feeding their illness and being consumed by it. They want the whole world to sympathize with their sickness. They seem almost proud of themselves if they have a rare disease, as if it was proof of their being unique! Would that they might give as much attention to health and well-being, our true heritage.

We need to know when we're happy, when we're well. If you identify with health, health will be your reward. But if you bring your attention to sickness, worshipping illness and disease, then you will reap accordingly. This is the choice we confront at all times: sickness or health. Knowing this, we have no alternative but to make the right selection. That which we choose and pay homage to, we will attract, with all the necessary component parts. What are you paying attention to? Are you focusing on your headache or are you focusing on what it feels like not to have a headache?

You want to select health. You want to select love. You want to select beauty, joy, and peace. All of these qualities operate in a healthy body and produce a different you. A healthy attitude brings about greater freedom from within by loosening and removing tensions and worry that promote illness.

Notice how doctors, perhaps unbeknownst to themselves, postpone comment on a patient's condition until the following morning? "Let's see how the patient is after a good night's rest," they often say.

I don't think they are consciously aware of the natural healing process, even when they credit rest and sleep for the patient's recovery. In itself, it's true, but there is more. While the patient is asleep the conscious mind is removed. The subconscious mind, which knows only healing, takes over. And provided it is left alone, without interference from the negativities of the conscious mind, healing takes place. Particularly in a hospital, surrounded by death and illness, a patient can accumulate a tremendous amount of doubt and fear. But these are removed when the patient is asleep, and the positive action of the subconscious has a chance to work in its natural way, which is health.

The power that created us is the power that heals us. All healing forces are within each of us. The natural healing process is in accordance with higher law. Each atom of the body and each reflex of the mind is attuned to an awareness of the infinite intelligence. This intelligence is within each atom and cell. The power is within.

A Search for a Doctor

We can't always interpret everything in specific terms, as it is happening, but we can sense when we're moving in the right direction. We will see the meaning of an experience more precisely at a later point.

No matter what takes place, know enough to see it as a blessing in your life. You might miss some things that can only be seen and interpreted in retrospect, all the little details and how they fit together. But while it is happening, recognize the possibility that perhaps a higher intelligence is guiding you.

When Adina auditioned for a Broadway play, it was on extremely short notice. The agent called on a Friday. The audition was to be held on Monday. In the meantime, Adina needed a social security number and working permit. In order to get the permit, I had to produce a health certificate. This meant I would have to get the certificate on Saturday.

As an infant, Luana had a pediatrician on a regular basis. With Adina, this was not the case. Because of what I'd learned, I felt we had less need for such services. But here I was, in need of a children's doctor. I started out Saturday morning knowing full well that I was going to get the health certificate. After all, how difficult could it be? First I went to Luana's pediatrician's office. Though he was out that day, his partner was there. He said I would need an appointment and that the first available would be in two weeks. He wanted to know if Adina had all her shots. I said, "All you have to do is look at her and you'll see she's perfectly healthy."

"We don't work that way," the doctor replied. "You need an appointment. I can't just look at her. We have to bring her records up to date. Certain tests have to be run." He went on and on. I said, "Good-bye and good luck."

From there I went to ten different pediatricians and received the same response. Most of them wouldn't talk to me because Adina wasn't their patient. I went to several hospitals, to different clinics, and I covered all the professional buildings. Making the rounds, I discovered all manner of specialties: "We don't handle that, we only handle this," or "For that you need a general practitioner." Well, try to find a general practitioner! There is no such doctor anymore. Nowadays they are all specialists of one sort or another.

I couldn't believe this was happening to me. I had started out *knowing* I was going to obtain the health certificate. There was no doubt in my mind. But by now, frantic in my quest, I was beginning to say to myself, "It looks like I'm not going to get it after all." It seemed so unreal not to get such a simple document. By late afternoon, I had all but given up.

It was almost 5:00 P.M. when I rang my last doorbell. I had become so experienced that when the nurse opened the door I asked her, "What kind of specialist do you work for?" She replied, "Ear, nose and throat." I was thinking to myself, "Well, obviously he's not going to see us," when the doctor appeared. "What seems to be the matter?" he inquired.

I proceeded to tell him my day's adventures. "Take a look at my child," I said. "She's the picture of health," which was obvious.

"Come in," he said. I could hardly believe it. "What's your name?" he asked Adina. "How old are you?" He covered all the formalities. Without examining her, he wrote out the certificate. I could see I was dealing with an intelligent man. After he wrote out the paper, he began the examination. Being a specialist, he could not resist his own specialty. "Have you had difficulty hearing?" he asked, after probing her ears with a variety of instruments. I had never noticed that she had any trouble hearing, yet Adina nodded. He continued poking with his instruments. Then he started removing an accumulation of wax so large that I began to wonder how she had heard at all.

Now I felt that I had been led to this doctor specifically. First, because I *knew* that I would get the certificate. But more importantly, because of our need for this particular specialist, I had gone through an entire day of doctor hunting, ostensibly for a health certificate, finally to find the right man to fill both needs. It had taken us all day to arrive at the right spot at the right time, for up until 5:00 P.M. this doctor had had a full schedule of patients. Adina and I appeared at the most propitious moment, just as he was about to close his office for the day. Everything worked out in a way that no one could have rehearsed, prepared, or anticipated beforehand.

During the course of the day, I had become increasingly keyed up. I was charged with negativity. I couldn't believe our predicament. I was irate about the entire medical profession. Toward late afternoon, my doubts were at their peak. I was ready to let go of the whole thing. "Maybe Adina's not meant to get the certificate." I almost gave up. My ego was getting the best of me. Exhausted, I let go. And lo and behold, the intellect moved out of the way, and I found even more than I came looking for. I said to the doctor what I always say when these things happen: "I was led to you by God." I don't care how they look at me. They may think I'm strange, but it's true. There is no other explanation. This type of experience reveals the guidance we continually receive from the higher intelligence.

Additionally significant, I think, is the business of medical specialties, breaking the body down into separate parts. Finger experts, throat experts, foot experts, you name them. This fragmentation is something to be examined. The proclivity of the time is to separate everything. We separate our bodies from our minds, our minds from our souls, as if they were entities unto themselves. We deal with everything as fragments. Then we continually struggle to gather these separate pieces back into a whole. The premise is wrong. We are whole beings to begin with. Our body, mind, soul—they are all one!

The unity is broken down even further by the human mind as concerns the body: leg cramps, headaches, chest pains, backaches, and so on. As if the body was comprised of spare parts rather than being an entity unto itself. That's where we need to start: to consider ourselves one. This is the unity that is all-essential to partake of life properly.

HEALTH IS LOVE

Observe healthy persons. You will see that they are exuberant with life. Observe a sick person and you'll find bitterness, resentment, and self-pity. Health comes down to one word: *love!* It is love that gives us our longevity, our well-being, our everything. With love, the impossible becomes possible, even growing new teeth or new hair, anything to make the body whole. It is whole, but unexpressed love distorts the truth.

We are whole, we are complete. It is the personal misusage of the mind that forever deals with all the so-called different parts. In actuality we are total to start with, we simply have not identified ourselves as such, because we're too busy with a part of this and a part of that. We're forever in the process of "getting it together."

By not expressing love, we separate ourselves from the

whole, and through our own distortion produce a false condition in the body. This condition is the symptom which the medical profession treats, but which it can never cure as long as it deals with symptoms instead of causes. There is nothing to cure. There is something new to cause in your life that is based on truth and on health. Once this is understood, the condition that manifested the symptom will now disappear into the nothingness it came from. It is important to know that you can always do something about your health or anything else in your life for that matter.

Begin with the reminder that you have not expressed love. Love is all there is and will ever be. All else is an illusion—*maya*. Love is the reason for our being here. I mean love in its true sense and not exclusively between man and woman, or parent and child. There must be love in everything we do and touch. At the supermarket, on the street, on the job, at home—no matter where you are—your attitude and your expression of love is continually involved. If it isn't, your mind begins to distort, and this will manifest itself in bodily ills later on. You can't escape the corresponding consequences, the cause-and-effect.

Love is patient; love is kind; love is forgiving; love does not brag; love is not jealous; love does not seek glorification; love can not be provoked; love does not and cannot linger over a wrong; love rejoices in the truth; and love accepts everything readily. Love is God. If you have the gift of prophecy and know all the mysteries and have all knowledge and faith but do not have love in your heart, you are nothing.

If someone complains to you, "I have a headache" or "I have a backache," tell him, "Hey, you look terrific." Watch how he perks up. All his features lift and his stance is different. A glimmer comes into his eyes, and the whole person no longer has the sickly look that accompanied his rehearsed complaints of a second before. Because you have placed your attention on his well-being, he begins to live up to your expectations. For that moment, having forgotten his woes, he can now experience himself as healthy.

Tell somebody "You look wonderful," and in an instant a glow comes over her. She becomes giving and full of love. In a flash, she is transformed into a beautiful being. There's a different person across from you, who is responding to the beauty you have glimpsed in her. She cannot help but react to that. From a downcast look, her features raise up, producing a radiant smile that lifts her face, and with it, the spirit. With that change in expression comes a change in her totality.

In all our communication with people, if it be not of an inspirational nature, it is best to remain silent. The greatest love you can give people who are sick is not to sympathize with their distorted condition. That merely feeds the illness. Sympathy strengthens negativity. The most creative mental work we can do is to look at sick persons and deny the seeming reality. See them with your inner eye in their ought-to-be state of health, the way they truly are. In doing this, you help them restore themselves to harmony. They will pick it up intuitively, telepathically.

A woman who had been coming to me for some time was given a projection of her father's impending death. Seriously ill, he had been hospitalized for several weeks. He had given up on life. The woman loved her father deeply, as did the rest of her family. She wanted to know how she could help him recover, even though doctors dismissed the possibility.

"How can I help him?" she asked me. "How can I inspire him to live?" I gave her a program to follow: "Look at your father. See him as he was in his prime. Hold that picture of him. See him happy, healthy, living life fully." I told her to go to sleep at night with that image in her mind and to wake up with that same picture. Visualize his radiant health every day while sitting with him in the hospital. It had never occurred to her before to disallow the seeming reality and to thereby cause a new reality. With difficulty, she convinced the other members of her family to stop sympathizing. They all set to work on visualizing their beloved father leading a normal, healthy life.

Within two weeks, her father had recovered. He left the hospital with a new outlook on life. The creative power, a wordless mental process, had evoked its own response.

That is the power of love.

CANCER

We are so much more than we think we are, yet we tend to set ourselves the hardest tasks. We are brutal, our own worst judges. This struggle within self is nonstop, evoked through our own self-contempt and our constant judgment. What we create in the world and the lives we touch, we forever weigh on a scale of good or bad. That which we have meted out to ourselves or others, our behavior, determines what we know and feel we must balance out for our own peace and harmony.

We misuse ourselves so much. We think so little of ourselves, really, and don't accept ourselves sufficiently. We're constantly belittling, demeaning our roles in life. To what degree do you accept yourself? The answer to that is an excellent indication of your inner workings.

We rarely treat ourselves lightly; we're actually cruel; in effect, we are our own worst enemy. From this point of reference we judge everything we encounter and therefore we deal harshly with life as well. That tears us apart, deteriorates the body, and shortens our lives.

Do you know that, on the average, it takes twenty years for cancer to manifest? Twenty years! Think about it. The nature of this disease is that the bad cells in the body eat healthy ones. People suffering from cancer must go through terrible mental distortion, eating away at themselves in order to bring about this evidence in their body. Look how long it takes, how hard one has to work against nature— twenty years of wrongdoing against the fibers of one's own physical being.

Contracting this disease has become something of a popularity contest nowadays. Prominent men and women give testimonials of their bouts with cancer, as if it were perfectly normal, an everyday occurrence. The public is besieged with information that cancer is a fact of life. "It must be detected early." "Know the seven danger signals." "Examine your breasts and look for lumps." Mass-thinking and the voice of authority are repeatedly calling attention to malignancy, and it has become instilled so deeply, people unconsciously prepare and condition themselves to attracting the disease. Before you know it, millions will have accepted it as a normal condition, when in fact it is an abnormality. To begin with, we must deal with what *causes* cancer in the body. Then we can effect healing.

Even some of the so-called evolved people who profess to higher spiritual attainment, even they are subject to bodily ills such as cancer for a variety of reasons: either through their own example to make the disease respectable; or en route to enlightenment, they have erred along the way. Or both. A third possibility is that through their ultimate self-sacrifice, they hasten a healing for the planet. Perhaps that is the case with many gurus and advanced spiritual teachers who have chosen this fate.

You'd be surprised how many things shown on TV are metaphysical. For example, many situations portrayed on medical dramas especially, or other shows, are very often related to misconceptions of the mind. The mishaps that occur in characters' lives are in direct correspondence to their inner conflict; the plots merely externalize the distortions in their minds. The character dying from cancer, for instance: before the cancer is evident, we learn about his personality.

He has the precise traits that produce cancer—bitterness toward self, resentment toward others, and an unwillingness to reconcile anything. Like everything else, cancer begins and ends in the mind.

HEALTH IS YOUR MIRROR

Your body, your physical being and appearance, is the direct result of your thinking-feeling experiences not only from this present lifetime, but shaped and accumulated from many lives before. Lifetimes of thinking and feeling are imbedded in every individual.

Accordingly, you are either healthy or sick, beautiful, homely, deformed, chiseled or flat-featured, fat, thin, short, tall, or what-have-you. You don't realize the important part you mentally play in this physical process. Your body does not act of its own accord, as a separate entity. It responds to your inner world.

Think about it: The condition of your body, even your shape and looks, constantly mirror your inner-world. Your mental conception of yourself directly affects your physical being. When the concept of self is negative, it literally tears down the fibers of your body. But when your concept of self is positive, creative, you are unified with the scheme of nature. You are in a process of continual renewal and health.

Learn to recognize that negativity, fear, hatred, and an unforgiving heart cause physical disorder. The creative process of life produces new cells all the time, and in such multitude we can't even count them. If we could remain in a positive state of mind for nine consecutive months, a complete transformation of body would result. Instead, we let our minds tear at our flesh, interfering with the natural process, and slowly killing the body.

Everything comes back to your state of mind and feelings.

Your features are formed by the way you think and conduct your life. Your physiognomy changes accordingly. Not long ago I ran into someone I hadn't seen in twenty-five years. I recognized her but her face was markedly changed. She used to have very clear, sharp features, but now they were flattened and blurred. In a flash I could see that she had spent a quarter of a century in a vacuum, in nothingness, and her features had altered correspondingly. Everything we think and feel registers in our faces and bodies, in our movements, gestures, and behavior. What we are is written all over us. *We* are responsible for the way we look.

By examining the inherent nature of any particular feature and its function, you will find that everything talks to you—and your features are remarkably articulate. A long nose, for instance, might belong to a person who meddles. A pug nose, pointing upward, bespeaks a very optimistic person, but one who doesn't take life too seriously. A broad, strong, straight nose indicates a person of strong will and determination.

Eyes are all-important, for they are the windows of the soul. By looking at someone's eyes, you can assess the level of consciousness. Dull eyes would likely belong to a person bored with life . . . glittering eyes, to an enthusiastic person, with an attitude of expectancy toward life. Deep-set eyes indicate a furtive, secretive nature. Round eyes are wide and open to experience. A sloe-eyed person may not see the larger perspective of things. Bushy eyebrows denote stubbornness. Eyebrows sloping downward indicate a negative outlook.

Observe someone's hands. Fleshy hands with chubby fingers indicate a shallow person who doesn't think things through. Long slender hands with flexible fingers belong to an artist; cold, clammy hands to a sickly nervous person. Hands with heavy veins indicate sensitivity. A firm, well-proportioned, solid hand is a healing hand.

Your body and features clearly describe your inner feelings, and you can change them according to the way you live. If your legs are swollen, it signifies a lack of understanding, a reluctance to listen to others, a stubbornness about new ideas. When you begin to understand and work on changing your *thinking-feeling* nature, your legs will return to their ideal proportion.

You can do something about anything and everything in your life. If you are overweight, a widespread problem these days, learn to love yourself. Most overweight conditions are an indication of a love-starved individual. Accept yourself and nurture yourself with love. Start with that and the desire toward self-indulgence will cease. You will find that you no longer have a craving for excess food. It's not enough for others to love you. Love can be given to you, but you cannot truly receive it until you love yourself.

THE SYMBOLOGY OF AILMENTS

Often we hear "You are what you eat," not realizing what it actually means. On the surface, it refers to the quality of food consumed. Yet our most vital food is what we think and feel. It is not what we eat that determines our appearance or demeanor. It is the quality of the total being— our thinking and feeling—that raises consciousness and produces health.

People are what they think and feel. Specific areas of the body and their symbology, in metaphysical terms, reveal the inner workings of each individual.

Eyes are for seeing. Trouble with your eyes obviously means that you are not perceiving and understanding things in your life as well as you should. People with vision problems often look for defects, look to criticize, see the wrongs in others, and quite possibly lack understanding of themselves.

Ears are to hear with. Hearing failure is directly connected with something the person doesn't want to hear. It hurts them, they don't wish to understand. Self-pity and pain enter in, hearing and not liking, because of the fear of confrontation. Listening attitude is also important. For instance, are you receptive to what you hear? Ask yourself, "Why don't you want to hear it?"

See how easy it is to connect? All it takes is simple intelligence and association to interpret a basic symbology that we all really know.

Trouble with *teeth*? Frivolous, compulsive talking without substance or consideration for others. Gossip.

The *voice* and *throat*? Truthfulness. If you're constricted, hoarse, or have laryngitis, what nonsense have you spoken to another, or to yourself? The voice is expression. Have you expressed yourself honestly?

Hands can reveal a variety of problems. Hands are your giving: either not giving to another, or to yourself. Examine in what way you give: for profit, seemingly doing the right thing for self-glorification? Or openly, lovingly, giving freely of yourself without expecting reward?

Arms are your faith: A condition or disorder of the arms, such as bursitis, may reveal a lack of faith, a loss of touch with God.

Arthritis and *rheumatism* are currently epidemic. These sufferers are usually rigid types, in constant conflict within themselves, always thinking they are right. They rarely let go. Animosity, negative attitudes, hatred toward others (or self), not forgiving another (or self), hanging on instead of releasing . . . everything we do wrong we pay for with our own flesh. By hating another, we are actually damaging the fibers of our own body.

The *spine* is our backbone. "No backbone" means you're weak, spineless. Common complaints of the lower back— lumbago, sacroiliac disorders, slipped discs—are the result of emotional insecurity, of unrequited love, and lack of personal fulfillment. Often, the mind becomes preoccupied with money matters and soon back disorders manifest. There is a definite correlation between emotional and financial security and back problems.

The *legs* are your understanding. What does it take to

stand on your own two feet? An enormous understanding of yourself—that you can be independent; that you have the strength, the resources, to stand on your own, to keep your feet on the ground. As people grow "older," they often have trouble with their *knees, legs, veins, feet,* and so forth, because their whole structure is crumbling; their understanding begins to falter, the future is projected with fear.

Lungs are the breath of life. Because we are living in a time when cancer is legion, we are constantly bombarded with messages equating smoking with the disease. If you feel that way, you certainly should give up the habit at once because you will likely attract lung cancer. It is what you feelingly attach to what you're doing—your attitude to the thing itself—that will produce corresponding results in your life. It is far more psychological than chemical.

If you enjoy smoking and attach nothing negative to it, chances are cigarettes won't hurt you. The only thing that will affect your body is your mind. It's not just simple, isolated thoughts, but thoughts accompanied by feelings. When we think and feel, we project a picture on a mental screen, an entire story in a flash, intensified by feelings, as we visualize our thoughts. This is then impregnated into our subconscious mind, indelibly written there, so that what you see and feel, you eventually produce in your life.

Heart trouble generally involves loss of love and feelings unexpressed. These feelings are trampled, smothered, frustrated, and constricted. "Heartache" literally means heart condition and people often die of broken hearts.

Blood disorders also have to do with love. Lack of love for self, for God, and in turn, lack of love for others. High and low blood pressure, leukemia, and diabetes all cry out to you: Love is all there is. Give love or else the system is poisoned.

Stomach, digestive tract ailments, and *ulcers* are almost always associated with aggravation, minimizing of self, not getting one's way, and eating your guts out. There is also a deep-seated fear of failure and an inner sense of disappointment. Stomach people hold onto old hurts; they never let go. This is a lesser form of devouring the self through guilt and bitterness, the forerunner of cancer. These sufferers often believe themselves to be all-knowing: "Everyone is an idiot and I'm so smart."

If someone comes for a reading and I see difficulty with ulcers, I tell them, "Never mind what you eat. Your attitude must be relaxed and harmonious; otherwise, even bland food will turn to acid." Again, the spirit in which you enter into things determines the outcome. If you're full of hostility, if something is eating at you, you're begging for an ulcer. How can you digest food if you can't make peace with your inner self? Your body is the outcome, the result of what you have thought and felt through the years.

Appendicitis is often an attack of hate and resentment.

Kidney stones or *bladder conditions* frequently indicate poisonous thinking about self or other people: greed, selfishness, criticism, anxiety, worrying, and bitter thoughts. The cure is right thinking, getting rid of the old (passing the stone), and moving on to the new.

The *liver* stores toxins and bile. Liver maladies most often are directly connected with bitterness in relation to self. *Hepatitis* and other conditions of the liver revolve around an accumulation of guilt, personal wrongdoing, self-conflict, and dissipation over an extended period of time. Liver problems are common among homosexuals, possibly because of internal conflicts, indecisive roles in life, and, in many cases, lack of honest self-confrontation.

Constipation and *rectal problems* are related to the past. What are you holding onto and not getting rid of? You'll find that so-called older people are frequently constipated. Why? Because they haven't had a new idea in God-knows-how-many years. Not only do they resist change, they literally live in the past. The past is their life, and living, reliving, and getting stuck back there produces constipation.

Lately, on TV, there are an endless number of laxative commercials in which constipation is referred to as "irregularity." Over and over again we are hypnotized into believing that when we reach a certain age, constipation is to be expected. We are being programmed for irregularity. And the actors in the commercials are no longer gray-haired: they're getting younger and younger, and soon masses of people of all ages will fall into the trap of irregularity.

When someone tells you he has a *headache*, ask him who gave it to him. Headaches usually connect with someone else saying things that annoy and irritate us, just as too much alcohol and disagreeable food will produce a similar effect. Many people suffer from migraines, which gives even stronger evidence of deep-seated feelings of being wronged or wounded by what others say. It is the martyr syndrome.

Dizziness is synonymous with mental confusion, imbalance, frustration, and bafflement within.

Insomnia is brought on by worrying about yesterday and tomorrow. Loss of identity in a today situation. As we become older (not necessarily in years, but in thinking), we begin to fear that time is running out. We become afraid to go to sleep, unconsciously fearing that we might not wake up. We are also fearful of confronting ourselves subconsciously, in the dream state.

Hair is the crowning glory of faith. When someone suddenly goes gray, chances are they have turned away from or abandoned an aspect of their faith. A person who suddenly or gradually turns gray and still has a lot of hair, is a person who at one time expressed a lot of faith in something higher or larger than the self—perhaps innately. Then he moved away from an expression of faith to material things and his attitude became more self-centered. This doesn't mean that his faith has been totally lost, however, because in that case there would be no hair left at all. It's also possible that baldness may not be attributable to a loss of faith in this lifetime alone. (Baldness may of course have other causes, such as vitamin or other dietary deficiencies or disorders in the circulatory system.)

Boils are a boiling disposition; they are rebellion, anger.

Breaking out of the *skin* is often a direct carryover of promiscuity from a previous life. You see it in adolescents, so it has to be a carryover, because by and large they are still in a virgin state. When it continues into later life, with permanent pockmarks, it may well indicate more than promiscuity—possibly even devilish behavior in a former incarnation.

You can trace almost everyone's inner workings, including your own, by such observation. Skin tone, eyes, posture, discomforts, parts of the body that are ailing tell you right away the underlying process of thinking and feeling. It is your day-to-day disposition that, taken on the average, determines your general state of health. The evidence in turn is recorded by the body, and an entire case history of a person can be revealed at a glance.

I was once at a dinner party where the host began discussing his mother's heart trouble. Not knowing anything more than that about her, I began to describe her characteristics, the way she shut out people, her inability to express love and to communicate with others, and her constant fault-finding. Intrigued, he asked, "When did you meet my mother?" I answered, "The moment you mentioned heart trouble."

DISEASES, BIRTH DEFECTS, AND KARMA

Every era has its own disease. In the last century, it was consumption; now it's cancer. Mass-thinking, of course, is certainly involved; but it also deals with reincarnation. Cancer is a predestined group karma, expressing itself as a particular disease that eats away the inner person. There is constant talk of wiping out certain diseases. Science is always on the verge of a breakthrough. But a hundred years from now, another disease will be prevalent to evidence a new karmic cycle.

Even though something is predestined, once you understand the karmic law fully, you no longer come under its influence. Civilization may be hypnotized en masse, but individually we can extricate ourselves. When you understand anything totally, you are able to let go and are no longer subject to the consequences of a karmic disease. It has no bearing on your life.

Different childhood diseases appear for different generations at a given time. Mumps, chicken pox, scarlet fever, tetanus, small pox, measles, and polio are carryovers from past lives that group together in certain karmic cycles. Almost all blood disorders against which children are given immunization shots are karmically related to immorality, because most everything negative pertaining to blood deals directly with love that has been abused. Leukemia, the extreme blood disorder, very likely expresses the extreme of such abuse in a past life.

Childhood diseases are direct reminders of where these souls have been in recent incarnations. You may come in with a condition that later disappears, indicating a less serious karmic implication. But if such a condition persists throughout your life, not only haven't you worked on yourself then, in a past life, you are repeating the same behavior now, without touching on the karmic debt still hovering over you.

Not every child is subject to these ills, however. Some have never had any immunization shots at all yet were never subject to any childhood disorders. This is because their parents did not identify with the diseases, thereby removing them from the realm of possibility. The parents remained uninfluenced by mass-thinking. The notion of disease was never accepted into their minds, nor introduced into their children's minds. An infant, up to age seven, comes totally under the influence of his or her parents or other similar authority figures such as daycare providers, teachers, and adoptive or foster parents. If the child gets sick, the parents have likely introduced illness into the youngster's experience. For example, parents are forever telling their children, "Don't sit in a draft. You'll catch pneumonia." The parent, genuinely believing the thought, introduces the idea into the young mind. The child is then likely to contract the illness as an actual experience. On the other hand, if the child is healthy, the parents identify with health, either consciously or innately.

There are karmic influences, however, that manifest before age seven in certain tendencies and leanings on the part of the child who enters this world with a colicky disposition, or susceptibility to diarrhea or allergies.

Once you recognize and understand the total workings of karma and the law of attraction you can do something about everything.

A certain woman, I'll call her Ruth, has been coming to me for several years now. About two years prior to the birth of her first child, it was indicated that the infant would need serious medical attention for the first few years of his life. When the child, a boy, was born, he came into the world without a mouth. Other features were misplaced. The nose was in the wrong spot, and the entire facial structure distorted. Unquestionably, this is a most traumatic situation for a mother to accept, even if she sees the karmic implications. It's still an incredible weight. In the case of Ruth it helped her to know that karma was directly involved with both mother and child. This understanding opened a new channel to working things out. Within two years plastic surgeons had performed wonders. An entire reconstruction of the child's face was undertaken and every feature found its proper placement. There are still difficulties to surmount. The child is now being taught to eat. The speech organs are being rebuilt. But Ruth informs me that the doctors predict her child will be perfectly normal within a few years.

She also told me that the initial reading remained her greatest source of strength throughout these difficult times. When the doctors revealed the birth deformities, she had been somewhat prepared. Truly, one can never be totally prepared for something so horrendous, but Ruth was better able to view the tragedy from a higher point of understanding. Not that she didn't fall apart at times. She simply managed to cope and handle her plight more compassionately. Now she looks ahead optimistically, knowing her child will eventually lead a normal life. She holds fast to this knowledge.

Through subsequent readings, something else became known to her; the possibility of perfect health. Ruth's identification with that concept, even under such painful circumstances, brought her to a larger understanding. Knowing that health was a possibility, she no longer saw the situation as devastating. Her self-blame diminished as her love of self and her infant increased. She continues to work on herself affirmatively and positively. She knows her child's life will normalize and that this enormously difficult period will fall into the past and be no more.

When a child comes into the world afflicted, in the innocence of infancy, he or she is an immediate reminder of where that soul has been in its past life. The karmic debt can't be ignored.

Suppose a child enters this life with a disease or physical disorder. That soul may have been healthy in a previous incarnation, yet with little compassion for people who were ailing. The child's condition in this life is a *direct connection* with the past. Compassion is inherent in all of us: feelings for others, the sense that the other person is us. Perhaps the afflicted soul experienced human tragedy without compassion in a previous incarnation. It may have passed up an opportunity to help the sick and afflicted, and so it begins a new life span *wanting* and *needing* to experience personal sickness and infirmity. Because it denied human feelings while in perfect health, the soul selects its own tragic encounter in order to suffer and balance out what it previously ignored, scoffed at, abused, or mistreated in others. The law of karma is constantly at work.

The soul requires experience to enlarge its understanding and to free itself from the karmic burden of previous lifetimes. A soul coming in with any kind of disorder can, by understanding karmic law, recognize its opportunity. When you fully realize that you have designed your circumstance, you can see it for what it is. You no longer need disease. You've paid your karmic debt and health becomes yours.

The road is always wide open. You can erase karma through conscious, deliberate selection. "All right, I came in with this or that problem. I understand why I made this choice and now I can eliminate it and testify to the truth of health, which I am." I've seen many such cases. I had a friend who was born asthmatic. She had lived with the condition all her life. How she pampered herself, how she enjoyed and took advantage of her allergy. One day, in her forties, she said "I don't have to have this condition any longer. I don't need it." She directed her conscious attention to health. Within a couple of weeks she was free of asthma.

These are the challenges we want to embrace. We can accomplish anything by understanding the motivating power that connects us with the continual flow of life. The symbologies of various illnesses and their physical locations are forever talking to us. If you were born afflicted, it is likely symbolic of where or what you were in a previous life. You have selected your difficulties in your essence state of being. Your physical self is your reminder of your choice. Once you make the connection you are a virtual powerhouse in what you can be and accomplish.

A CROSS-EYED LITTLE GIRL

As children, we are natural beings. We are what we are, and that's all, in the honesty of childhood, in the act of being ourselves. It is strange for children to be surrounded by sickness. They have no concept of illness. Innately, a child rebels when confronted with the guilts and responsibilities sick people impose. When, for example, it is thrust on them that "Mother is sick. Don't be unruly, noisy, and inconsiderate." Children, by nature, identify with health. Sickness is foreign. We are all born with a blind belief in a higher power, with a faith that has no explanation.

When I was four, I was cross-eyed. It first became visible at age two. My parents had gotten me glasses (which didn't work at all) to adjust my eyes. I remember before going to bed every night—bear in mind I had no conception of religion or anything—I would pray to God that my eyes would be straightened out. I *knew* that through God this sort of a miracle was possible.

When I started school at five, the other kids ridiculed me because of my glasses. By the second year, I was determined not to have to wear them. I prayed incessantly, and I entered into a bargain with God: "God, if you're really there—and I know you must be—you'll make sure that I can throw away these glasses. And for that, I will be a good girl. This way, I will know that you exist." I was an extremely wild, rebellious, and unruly child, so a promise to be good was a monumental sacrifice.

I visited an eye doctor regularly to check my eyes, and each time he looked at them, he'd say, "She has to continue wearing glasses." I hated them and refused to wear them. As a consequence I developed a system whereby I could voluntarily straighten my eyes but couldn't see. When straightened out, everything was blurred. By this time I had memorized the eye chart and could prove to the doctor I had progressed. During one visit, I straightened my eyes, faked reading the chart, and said triumphantly, "I'm not going to wear these glasses anymore. I don't need them." He agreed that I could cut down on their use.

One day I went to school without them. My classmates

had always seen me with glasses, and now I became the center of attention for a new reason. I could see if I crossed my eyes, but I couldn't see when I straightened them. Every time they would look at me, I would straighten my eyes to show them I was as normal as anyone. If I thought they were not looking, I would cross my eyes and quickly take in whatever I could.

I didn't realize it was a whole exercise I was doing with my eyes. Because I had a terrible complex about being ridiculed, I was forever straightening my eyes. When the teacher asked me to read something from the blackboard, I would quickly cross my eyes and then straighten them again, because I knew the students were all looking at me. Within the year I actually began to see normally, without glasses and without crossing my eyes.

In a sense, this was miraculous. But was it? I entered into life with weak eye muscles, obviously having missed seeing and understanding something of importance in a previous life. I worked on it intuitively from some subconscious memory which dealt with a faith in something: that every thing is possible; that my eyes could be perfect. And so they came to be.

As a youngster I had many brushes with death, but was never afraid. No matter what the experiences were, they couldn't disrupt my belief that I was healthy and indestructible.

When I was five, my mother sent me across the street to get a cake from the bakery. I didn't want to go, but she insisted. I went unwillingly, angrily. Crossing the street, I was hit by a car. I got up bloody from head to toe, my glasses shattered. Right away a crowd formed, but I managed to escape them and run upstairs into my house where I locked myself in the bathroom. I wasn't in any pain. All I could think of was "I have to clean myself up so that nobody will know what happened."

Five minutes later, several neighbors and a policeman

rang the doorbell. My mother answered, and they told her that I had been hit by a car and should be taken to the hospital. She was quite confused and upset when I emerged from the bathroom. I didn't want anything to do with any of them. Nothing could drag me to a hospital because I *knew* I was all right. I never for a moment entertained the possibility that I was hurt, despite the crowd's hysteria.

Between ages five and six, I was hit by cars three different times, but was never really hurt and would never allow a doctor to touch me. Once I was playing with a group of boys and chased a ball into the street. A motorbike came racing by. With my unbelievable energy I ran straight into it, and the driver flew half a block into a ditch! I scampered away unhurt, worried only that he was going to be mad at me.

A child of this age is all subconscious mind and acts from memory, from innate knowledge. I had absolutely no fear of bodily harm; and I certainly did not sit down to consider things intellectually after only five years in this incarnation. My health was an instinctive knowing and nothing could disrupt it. Health is dependent on your state of mind. Youthfulness is a direct result of health.

THE FOUNTAIN OF YOUTH

If the mind was continually operating within the higher laws of intelligence, we would be in a perpetual state of youthfulness. We would not need, as was once my folly, a fountain of youth in the form of a European spa.

When I arrived in Badgastein, Austria, with my father (a trip I'll describe later) a thorough physical examination was mandatory. A staunch, dogmatic Viennese doctor went through various formalities in examining me while I laughingly insisted that I was in perfect health. After two hours he said, "You are in perfect health. What are you doing here?"

I told him that travel folders described Badgastein as a veritable fountain of youth, and I wanted to partake of their offerings. He asked what I had in mind, and I replied, "I want to look seventeen." I was twice that. He said curtly, "Impossible!" removing his glasses and really looking at me for the first time.

He was right. Badgastein was to be no fountain of youth. The accent on youth that is so prevalent in our country (and spreading elsewhere) is frightening. The approach limits us to age-numbers and is wholly one of deterioration. It deals only with outer illusion, bracketing according to age. A spiritual mind, a mind in totality with God, with love, will perpetuate youth. Youth is an integral part of the right state of mind which produces the right way of living. Because lines, wrinkles, and any forms of deterioration that signify age come from wrong workings of the mind, having and maintaining a right state of mind is the only effective way to stay youthful. Wrong thinking, worrying, the fear of growing old will only quicken and deepen the aging process—no matter how much time you spend at beauty parlors and spas.

You will notice that some people remain a certain age in terms of appearance: they never seem to get older-looking after a certain point. This is because they have come to something more within themselves which has arrested the manifestation of their chronological age. Significantly, *they express life more lovingly.* They don't play the numbers game.

A person in love suddenly looks much younger. There's a glow about love. Love immediately brings us into harmony with the higher intelligence. All the positive forces are realized. The newly born cells of the body operate freely, without interference from the negativities of the human mind. In this way, age dissolves. Persons in love love the world around them: they no longer pick it apart. Life is beautiful for them, and everything goes smoothly, whatever they encounter. They are in step with nature's rhythm.

The love which is so obvious in our lives when experienced on a one-to-one basis is the very love that we need to generate all the time. Not exclusively toward just another person; we need to generate it always, toward everyone and everything in our lives, *including ourselves*. There would be no aging! There would be no death! If there be such a thing as sin, not loving would be the greatest of them all, with accelerated aging and premature death as the punishment.

You cannot love another if you do not love yourself; and you cannot love yourself if you do not love God. It's as simple as that. Merely going through the motions will never do. Nor will living in exactly the right way or doing the so-called proper thing produce anything worthwhile, unless love be the force that operates in and through you all the time.

CHAPTER EIGHT

WHERE HAVE YOU BEEN?

*We are simultaneously the past, present, and
future. We are in a continual state of becoming.*

AN INCIDENT WITH A MEDIUM

People tend to look upon life as limited to the reality per-
ceived through the senses from the cradle to the grave.
"You're born to die; and in between its one big road of suffering, with an occasional pause for a moment of happiness."

Not too many years ago, I had a group of guests over for
the day. We were swimming in the pool. A good friend of
mine was discussing reincarnation. She felt that genius ex-
emplified it, as when certain individuals such as Bach,
Einstein, or Edison are born with extraordinary knowledge
or brilliant capacities. "Surely they would have to bring it
with them from a previous life." I'll never forget how I
looked at the others, as if to say, "Is she for real?" At that
time, although I had an abiding faith in a higher power, I
could not identify with reincarnation.

Soon afterward, someone took me to a séance. I had no
idea what a séance was, but I was certainly intrigued. At this
particular one, we were instructed to chant to arouse the
energies in the medium. Abruptly, her personality was removed and a horrible loud voice began to speak through

her. It was quite spooky and irritated me so much that all I could think of was how I was going to get out of there. She then came over to me and said—in that harsh voice, but a bit gentler— "To you I will have to speak much more softly, because my voice irritates you so." Immediately, I was a goner! I thought, "My God, she's picking my brains! Whatever is going on, *it knows!*" I hadn't uttered a word, the woman had never seen me before, and yet she was able to pick up my very thoughts.

In that same grating voice, she later singled me out again and began to speak about a piece of jewelry I kept in a drawer at home. It was an unusual and very detailed necklace, given to me by my mother, and she described it perfectly. I had never worn the necklace because it was too delicate. I was flabbergasted. How could she describe it when I'd never even worn it! She continued, telling me how my mother had come by this necklace and how my mother's father had given it to her in a European country. Then she described my mother, her traits, the country, the language— everything. Finally, she said that *all this was to let me know that life was eternal.* She wanted me to know that my mother's presence was there, and the knowledge of the necklace was proof of it. That gave me a jolt. I began to shiver. It was beyond all logic, beyond intellectual understanding.

A new door opened for me. Reincarnation, something I had never thought of, became plausible, something I would come to firmly believe in. My awakening dates from that experience. It was the beginning of my search for esoteric knowledge.

Most people have difficulty equating with the larger scale of life than we know here on Earth. Today I often encounter incredulity when I mention reincarnation. "Do you really believe all that?" skeptics will inquire.

"Do you remember when you were a month old?" I ask them. The answer is usually "No." "Does that mean that you were never an infant?" That's my favorite opener, when having lived before seems to them such an impossibility. It gives them a chance to probe deeper in to themselves, to think about the possibilities.

Because we cannot remember our past, does it mean that we never lived it?

REINCARNATION

It is believed that at one time the Earth and the moon were one. Life on the "moon" planet was in a lesser evolved human form, and there was no division of the sexes. Souls coming into incarnation at that time did not come through passage out of a womb; rather they were thrust upon the planet directly through the creative process of the higher intelligence. It is also believed that at that time all souls were totally dependent on the higher intelligence, God. There was no individual thought.

There came a time when the Earth and moon began to separate. Souls started to find their own free will through ego, and they also began to experiment with it. This ultimately affected the physical separation of the moon from the Earth, following the universal laws whereby the mental determines the physical. The Biblical account of Adam and Eve in the Garden of Eden, eating the fruit of the tree of knowledge, experimenting with right and wrong may refer to the separation of the moon from this planet. Or it may also refer to the separation of humanity from God. Human beings found ego and with it the beginning of the intellect and the power to reason. As a consequence, the connection with the Godhead was severed. Since that time, the human race has been in confrontation with the universe, rather than in accord with it. Temptation, doubt, pain, fear, loss of the absolute, and death are the results, to be experienced and re-experienced in the reincarnation cycles until the journey back to the Godhead is completed. With the separation of the sexes, we alternate between male and female from one incarnation to another. The punishment women came to suffer was giving birth and having to endure great physical pain. This punishment was a result of the separation of human will and ego from God.

We chose to separate ourselves from the Godhead, and have since embarked on a path seeking to regain our rightful place, unification with God through multitudinous reincarnational cycles. This is our journey home. This is our karmic origin. We start out whole, unified with God; then we experiment with free will. We discover through wisdom and reason that we must return to the infinite intelligence that we separated ourselves from; we must journey back by perfecting ourselves deliberately and consciously. And in making this choice, paradoxically, we exercise the height of free will. Given our present development and evolvement this journey back can only be accomplished through reincarnation—the path back to wholeness.

Certain cosmic events must be better understood in order to grasp more readily their bearing and influence on our lives. Even the Earth's separation from the moon was not the beginning. There is neither beginning nor end. This was merely one phase in the never-ending unfoldment of life in the universe. People have been attracted to the moon from time immemorial. Why this fascination? When we are unconsciously drawn to something, it is because a memory that arouses our feelings is triggered within us. Why are certain people romantically affected by the moon and its phases, while others are so frightened of it? The moon affects our moods, our emotions, but is its influence outer, reflective, and physical, or from within us? The answer is for each of us to probe.

Just as we, as human beings, evolve through our karmic deeds, so do we influence the Earth's own karmic evolvement. Earthquakes, floods, fires, volcanic eruptions; such devastating natural phenomena are the effects of our individual negativities—greed, materialism, lust for power—magnified on a global scale in mass killings and warfare.

The visual proof of our mass negativity can be seen in the changing face of the Earth. Not only in the altered topography or ecological imbalance, but also in the color tones of the planet's surface, which is turning to redder hues. The earth's karma is to eventually reunite with the moon and sun, just as we will reunite with the Godhead. Millennia from now, a planet called earth will be nonexistent. Astronauts walking on the moon, traversing space, make possible the impossible.

Reincarnation is the cycle of life and rebirth. It is important to understand this premise because it answers questions that cannot be resolved through other sources such as religion, philosophy, science, or the intellect. There is a very important phrase in the Bible: "Before Abraham was, I am." What does that actually mean? "I am that I am," or "Before Abraham was, I am," means that we have *been* all the time. Before Abraham, the oldest patriarch, even before his lifetime, *we were*. We have always been. We will always be.

This is one confirmation of reincarnation, but most religions don't accept this interpretation. They reject it, in order to maintain their hold on their followers. It would mean there's always another chance to redeem ourselves, at some future time, and religions can't afford to take that attitude. Most of them are based on fear. "If you don't do this or that, if you don't support the institution financially, you'll end up in hell!" You'll even find examples of such admonitions in the Bible. The Bible is not to be taken literally, however. It should be read and interpreted symbolically for its spiritual wisdom, bearing out the *essence-truth of cosmic intelligence* and its directives to humanity from the beginning to the end of man's earth existence.

The question is often asked, "Why do some people suffer when they appear to be innocent, never having committed a wrong? It seems so unjust, so unfair." We must understand that what we have done in previous lives has its bearings and results in this life, that we reap exactly what we have sown.

Unless we accept the premise of reincarnation, we will not be able to understand that we are navigating our own destiny. Through these continual cycles, we devise our own system of retribution, deeds we want and need to compensate for as our lives go by.

After many hours of sleep, we awaken to find the circumstances that connect us with our previous day. We grasp it all immediately, with a perfect sense of continuity. In the same way, we meet in this life what we have prepared for ourselves in between incarnations. Our life today corresponds to the actions of our previous lives. Everything that has gone before causes our birth into this life, into these particular circumstances, and at this very time. How we live today, in this incarnation, will become the cause of our subsequent lives.

We are what we are because of what we have been. Every moment of your living *right now* is affecting your next moment.

THE WORKINGS OF KARMA

For every force, there is a counter force. For every negative there is a positive. For every action there is a reaction. For every cause there is an effect.

Basically, there is only good karma, because it is all connected to our spiritual growth. This is good karma, because we get the chance to work out what we started in past lives. There is nothing fatalistic or rigid about karma; our own free will is constantly at play. We can accept or reject the opportunities that we come across in our lives which in a sense have already been set up by each soul from the cumulative activities of its prior incarnations.

The law of karma, which no one can escape but which everyone can work out, has at its root *love*. Through love there is no karma that cannot be resolved. With love, we learn to forgive ourselves, and in turn we learn to forgive everyone else we meet in life. We then become of service to every need in the world around us, thereby canceling our karmic debts.

We are irrevocably tied to anyone we have wronged at any time—in this life or in previous ones—until such time as we have righted that wrong, thereby releasing the other person and ourselves from this involvement. The subconscious mind remembers everything, every detail. Moreover there is the collective unconscious mind, where everything is recorded in what the Hindus refer to as the Akashic Records.

Inwardly, we crave to balance ourselves under karmic law. We cannot escape it. We mete out our own punishment, and unless we live helpfully and productively in this life, our next incarnation will perhaps turn out to be a lot worse than the present one. If you steal, your goods will be stolen from you (sooner or later, not necessarily within this lifetime). The murderer will have to die by violence himself, because "those who live by the sword shall die by the sword." Your every action will bring its own reaction.

The most exciting aspect is the fact that *we always have a choice.* By embracing and embodying the laws of karma, you work with the very principles which will erase and annihilate all karma. It starts the moment you forgive yourself and others, because with forgiveness you rid yourself of guilt and guilt is all-consuming. To forgive another soul is to free yourself of the hatred, anger, and resentment that tortures your soul and creates sickness in your flesh.

You must learn to forgive quickly. You should never go to sleep at night carrying the quarrels of the day. You must cleanse your subconscious mind of all negativities. This action should first take place in the conscious mind and then be directed toward the subconscious. Only then will it take effect.

Blaming other people is merely deterring you from loving yourself. If you examine the blame you place on others, it's primarily due to your resentment of yourself, which prevents the resolution of karma. We all need to learn to give and receive love, which puts us under the law of karma. This cannot be stressed enough: *If love is not involved in your actions, not only are you not working out your karma, you are building new karma into your future.*

There are many decent, respectable people who would never harm anyone. They exist in a nondescript, passive way. They neither hate nor love. The question is: Why are they here? And why are we? If we don't exert maximum effort in our walk in life and deliberately direct our energies toward karmic knowing, we are misusing our whole life. If we fail to engage actively in furthering our own person, life slips through our fingers in a wishy-washy way. We neither hurt anyone, but neither do we touch anyone.

No one can escape the immutable laws of cause-and-effect. That is the subject of our lessons each time we are here in an incarnation. Earth is truly our school, since it's really not our natural home. Jesus said, "I am in this world, but not of this world." An incarnation on this planet is like attending the highest "University." We are here to learn the eternal lesson of life itself, our connection with the cosmos. In between our visitations on Earth, we spend time on other planets in spirit form, in accordance with our needs and level of development, in preparation for our next incarnation. The instant the soul departs from this life, it reviews its entire Earth experience from the moment of death back through birth. Every wrong against another is relived with magnified intensity, as though the soul was the sufferer. The impact of the wrong committed is not merely glossed over but registered with even deeper magnitude. While in the spirit world, we live *within* the person we have wronged, not just feeling the pain and anguish we inflicted, but living it to the full. Based on what your soul experiences within another soul, you prepare the circumstances, conditions, challenges, and even the people that you will encounter in a subsequent life back on Earth.

In order to meet the appropriate conditions which we

need to attract to work out our karmic debts, our soul travels to different planets in the universe. Each planet has its own influence and our soul seeks out those that will best fortify it.

Whenever I think of my nephew, Amnon, I sense him as a burst of sunshine. His sunny disposition tells me he must have spent a lot of time on the sun prior to his arrival here. If someone is moody, or perhaps selfish or detached, chances are that person rested on Saturn for eons prior to coming into this life. Hitler must have brooded and fed on Saturn, as well as Mercury and Mars, before he incarnated here in his last life.

A soul entering an incarnation on Earth dons a physical body and is then subject to physical laws which cannot be ignored. However, a memory is retained of previous influences during the period between death and rebirth. The laws of the spirit-world and the laws of this planet are interwoven. Our intuition reminds the soul—through subconscious memory—of past lives. Desire for right action draws the soul toward its future.

All our previous lives determine our surroundings today, because the component parts are attracted to the nucleus set up by the individual soul in all its experiences. In every incarnation the soul attracts the right opportunities and conditions necessary for working out its karma. Through free will, the road chosen is subject to many variations.

Whether or not you believe in reincarnation is unimportant. The truth survives in and of itself and is not dependent on our conceptualization of it. Even if you think only in terms of a single lifetime, you still want to conduct yourself in such a way that you cause only good and love in your world. At least let that be the yardstick by which you live.

GROUP KARMA

The more realized and developed a soul is, the more carefully it will select the proper conditions to work out its karma. Souls determine each detail of their lives: country, climate, race, color, religion, parents, and even appearance. *Everything* is predetermined in the essence-state of being.

Why does a group of souls come in as blacks or as Jews or another oppressed minority in a difficult era, for instance? Many of these beings have to work out their own prejudice from prior incarnations; only some do so because of a particular spiritual mission for others. Prejudice and bigotry have been prevalent in society from time immemorial, in one form or another. The selection of a particular race—especially during a period of condemnation—is directly connected with previous lives. Often those who are the victims in the present period were formerly the oppressors or vice versa. Whatever the time period and particular pressures, certain souls have chosen this experience for themselves as necessary to learn what it is like to be on the receiving end of their prior blindness and injustice.

Every one of your prejudices clues you to what you have done in a previous lifetime. Bear that in mind in meeting these situations today. Let it trigger your memory. Treat others as yourself because you've been on the receiving end of this very same bigotry and oppression. In your mistreatment of others today you are preparing yourself to receive in kind in your next lifetime, if not sooner.

There are many different reasons an individual soul comes into life on this planet. There are some souls who come with tremendous purpose, to be of great service and example to the world. Almost all of us, however, come here with personal, individual karma that needs to be worked out reciprocally in connection with others. In this sense, genocide or mass murder of a particular race or religion might well be considered group karma. The explanation would almost have to be that the victims once played the oppressors in a previous period, and that which they caused to happen to others had to subsequently be experienced by them.

A madman such as Hitler may come into an incarnation a thousand years hence, totally crippled. Until then, in the spirit-world, his soul is doomed to go through the tortures and deaths that he inflicted on millions, living and feeling each experience of every victim. Back on earth, in a new incarnation, the world would view this crippled child, seemingly innocent, as a pitiful thing. "How could God create such an unfortunate being?" they might ask. Yet someday his soul will reincarnate, and the karma incurred in his life must inevitably be paid off. In not relating to these things sufficiently, we fail to comprehend why horrible things take place. It's not that we shouldn't feel compassion for the maimed or oppressed, quite the contrary. In our feelings of compassion, and our empathy and understanding of others, we perfect ourselves.

All of karma is a progression, moving in cycles toward the ultimate perfection of the human race. Oftentimes we seem to regress, but for good reason. Prejudice and bigotry are regressions, the accumulation of further karma. Still we can and *must* pay our debt here and now. The price is love and respect for the dignity of all life. There is no standing still. Even if you do nothing, you do not hate; yet, you do not love; still you are regressing and will have it twice as hard next time around.

There are certain situations where lives end abruptly and prematurely. War, for example, comes under both group karma and individual karma. Such group karma is not controlled by the individual, even though individual karma is at stake as well. Some deaths appear to be an external cutoff, yet the individual has partially prepared for an early demise in the essence-state of being. For these souls, the need to come back quickly is immense. Because of this need, they may come back into any situation, not properly selecting the conditions that would enable them to work out their particular karmic debts. Often, in these cases, the life experience may again be cut short or be extremely difficult. It takes a great deal of self-contemplation to enter into a life-span with a specific program, and this is not always done thoroughly. The result will be an even more hazardous return to earth next time around.

We are coming into an important period of time in terms of group incarnation. Many souls now taking foothold upon this planet are directly from the time of Jesus. That is why so many organizations are popping up, one after the other, under the banner of Jesus. All of these people connect with his time, and many are here now to bring into expression the essential spiritual values of life. But while some may come to exemplify the values Jesus stood for, others distort them. Just because people proselytize in the name of Jesus does not mean they necessarily follow his teachings. These souls may have been attracted to Jesus originally and not applied his ideals then, either. By the end of this century, however, more spiritually developed souls will incarnate to effect greater purification of these truths and bring them into actualization.

Periodically, new impulses are given to the earth from the spirit-world in order to accelerate mankind's growth. Such new impulses come at very specific times when earthlings have descended too deeply into matter: when human beings have degenerated and debauched themselves to sub-human levels; when we have wandered too far from the Godhead. The spirit-world expresses itself through extraordinary personalities, such as Shakespeare and Goethe in their time, or Rudolf Steiner in our own time period. These are but a few examples of such new impulses that contribute in their lasting influence on the humanities.

Moses, in his time, brought to mankind the laws of God, commandments necessary for that particular epoch, which endure today. Jesus Christ is the highest representation of the Godhead. Jesus brought the new love impulse to the world. The traumatic effects of this example will influence and serve us till the end-time of this planet earth. Such unique beings come to illuminate the world and to show the way as direct messengers from God.

Clues to Previous Lives

People are often fascinated by and identify with certain historical periods, particularly students of history whose strong preference for one era, time, or place draws them like a magnet. This is direct indication of their feeling a link with their own experiences in previous lives. The inklings aroused through a dormant memory are the clues. Why else would an individual be interested in events that took place thousands of years ago in China, for example? Because of subconscious memories of our own past lives. Or why our current interest in King Tut and Egyptology?

The rejoinder is always, "If I lived before, how come I don't know it?" Frankly, I believe that if most people fully remembered their past lives and deeds, they'd go crazy to the brink of suicide. They couldn't handle such material. Think of what psychiatry has to deal with in terms of just this one lifetime, just one childhood, which often cripples people emotionally. Imagine then unearthing and reliving dozens or even hundreds of life-spans. It would be devastating.

We glimpse only that which we are truly ready for. This kind of readiness is always in accordance with the individual's development and consciousness. It's not just a matter of waiting for it; it has to be arrived at through understanding. In a seance, it came through that I had once been the sister of Mohammed. There were many racial inequities between Arabs and Jews then, and I was told that I had incurred a heavy karmic debt in that incarnation. My father was in an incarnation at that time as a female servant in our household whom I mistreated. Examined in this light, I can better understand my great need to constantly please him—as if to compensate for prior wrongs. Look how many generations later, how many lives later, I find myself impelled—beyond logic—to right these wrongs. I can sense it in me; I can feel it in response to my behavior of long ago.

We are given many clues; we need only learn to read them. People who are born blind, for instance, were probably souls who were extremely prejudiced in a previous lifetime, did not see the plight of other people, and so wronged them.

If we understand the function of a part of the body, what it performs, we can better understand what it means symbolically in terms of health and life, both past and present. There is so much talking to us all the time. The clues are the same for all states of reality.

Sometimes it's possible to tell about people's past lives by their skin. Flesh tone, discoloration, elasticity, all of these offer clues as to where that soul was in a previous incarnation. Everything we feel and do engraves itself on our faces and on our bodies. Everything that we are, that we practice, is evident and is translatable. We can always change, however, whether it's a facial feature, skin tone, mental condition, sexual proclivity, or whatever.

You can notice in children signals of their karmic leanings in this lifetime, be they athletic, artistic, inventive, mechanical or domestic. Parents have the responsibility for guiding their offspring in the right direction through observing the child's leanings and potential. The symbology is often obvious. It can be readily seen and understood, triggering our intuitive memory, inspiring parents into working karma out with their children. By working with these clues, you can better help your children lead a balanced life.

When I was fourteen, I went to Egypt. It was wartime. I was invited as a guest of a girlfriend and her parents. When preparing for a trip, you usually try to imagine what it will be like. But whenever I thought about my destination, I could only sense an empty lot. I could not envision a house. Somehow I knew it wouldn't be there. When I arrived in Alexandria my friend's house was full of rubble and there was billowing smoke. I wasn't surprised when I was told the house had been bombed.

After settling in another house, my girlfriend and I went to the beach one day. We found a rubber raft and decided to take it out into the water. After drifting quite far from shore, it suddenly sprang a leak and the raft began to sink. I told her that I didn't know how to swim, and she said to me, "I can barely swim myself." She had to struggle for her own life, so I knew I was on my own. I started swallowing water, when suddenly it flashed through my mind that I was going to die! It all seemed so absurd, so unbelievable. I thought, "My God, is this a way to go? Is this all there is to life? I'm only fourteen!"

The next thing I knew, I woke up in a hospital. The English officer who owned the raft, an excellent swimmer, had seen our struggle from ashore and swam out to where we were, saving my life. My friend made it ashore on her own.

When you have a highly dramatic experience in a foreign country, it may well be directly related to a past life there. I felt this all along, but I couldn't explain it at the time. Later I was able to make the connection. The Englishman who saved me was unquestionably linked with me from a previous era in the Middle East. The British, who have been intrigued with and possessive of the Middle East, were clearly Semitic in an earlier time. Many of them became so intoxicated with the Arab world that they didn't want to return to England. T. E. Lawrence (of Arabia) would be the most outstanding example of this karmic attraction.

All the time I was in Egypt, everything was familiar. I felt quite at home there, though I had no real affinity for the average citizen. The language, the food, the customs, nothing seemed strange to me. It was as if I knew everything without being told. These are the hints of where we have been in the past.

THE SPIRIT-WORLD

In the spirit-world, depending upon its development, the soul can travel. If advanced, it can instantaneously project desire and bring it into reality. If an advanced soul wills itself into a situation, or a geographical location through imagination and visualization, it is there instantaneously. These are the laws of the spirit-world. In that dimension, conditions are different: The imaginative faculty is everything. That which is imagined and thoroughly visualized becomes the actual.

If a spirit is not quite as realized it is less mobile, not as free to roam. Such a soul is not yet working with the full potentiality of its own resources. In a sense, these same laws are evidenced here on Earth. If your level of consciousness is more realized, you are a freer being. Your imagination is demonstrated in your daily living. In the Earth experience, the physical body perceives many distractions through the five senses. This makes it more difficult and challenging to mentally visualize for ourselves. Greater and more deliberate effort is required on our part in order to transcend these obstacles.

Everything is the result of your consciousness, whether *here* or *there*. Even the shapes of spirits are quite different, based on their level of consciousness, much as we reveal ourselves by our features and bodies here on Earth. A fully realized soul will manifest in the shape of a perfect sphere and can travel without limitation. The level of consciousness before a sphere is an incomplete sphere. Such a soul is limited in mobility, but to some extent can still travel outside its own realm and dimension. The level prior to that is a cube; the level before that an incomplete cube, with areas not filled in as yet, aspects not harmonized. The less developed a soul, the greater the restrictions and the more the imperfection in the shape. Based on shape, souls can recognize each other's development. Before reaching the more geometric shapes, there are many stages a soul passes through, that appear blurred and indefinite. Soul shape can be likened to the various colors of auras that can be seen around people. The color and clarity of our auras reveal our state of development here on Earth.

A soul that is highly developed in consciousness in the spirit-world can appear here on this planet anytime it chooses. Many people claim to have seen Jesus, or other evolved souls who have special meaning for them. These souls materialize so completely that they can be seen by other enlightened beings. They are not limited to time or geography and can appear simultaneously in many places. This kind of realized soul knows no restrictions.

In the spirit-world, existence is much easier. There is an harmonious state of pure consciousness, whatever the level. Whereas in the physical form, in an Earth experience, we encounter problems and obstacles at every turn. We must seize them as the opportunities we need to work out our karma. It is for this reason that there is really no bad karma. If we recognize everything as existing for our advancement, then karma can only be good. Challenges, obstacles, and problems—these are vital food for us. Once we are on this planet, the testing begins. When you understand life from such a large perspective, then you welcome everything that comes your way—good or bad. We must all travel this road to become masters of our own destiny.

When an incarnation is over, the soul disconnects itself from the physical body and reviews the entire life span just ended, going back over every detail, starting with a third of one's life, that of sleep and the dream reality. As the incarnation unreels, the soul becomes the *recipient* of its deeds, feeling the pain, the injustice, as well as the good and loving involvements.

In our essence-state of being, devoid of body, the honesty with which we examine ourselves is total. We can clearly see if our actions were for our own self-aggrandizement, pleasure, egotism, material gain, or in service to others. More often than not, we would find that our thinking was primarily concerned with ourselves, with little consideration for other human beings. This alerts and consequently prepares us to exercise greater self-discipline, better behavior, and more love when in a subsequent incarnation.

The expression of love, constructive actions, compassion, and dignity are really the keys that unlock the kingdom of heaven within you. Those of us who go through life blindly, using force and anger, destroying instead of building, suffer corresponding consequences in their future incarnations.

We return to Earth many times until we have, without qualification, fully felt, fully experienced, and fully expressed love in the purest sense.

THE SOUL'S SELECTION

Every experience we go through is impressed and absorbed into our consciousness and plays its own significant part in our future. Each experience has different significance, depending on the conscious work we undertake in connection with it. The path toward enlightenment is unique for each of us.

We carry within ourselves the sum total of all our experiences, and this totality contains a potential of unlimited capacity. We carry this unique totality with us always, whether here on Earth or in the spirit-world. But when we're no longer in a physical existence and have freed ourselves of earthbound desires that literally chain us to this planet, we can see with greater clarity. We see our gains, and taking this into account, we fashion our future through our talents and capacities in preparation for another life-span. It is very important, therefore, what qualities a soul carries from this life into the spirit-world, and also what qualities it carries back into this earthly experience.

The laws of Earth cannot be found anywhere else. They are very difficult and very different from the laws of the Spirit-World. When Earth and Spirit-World laws become interwoven within us, they provide a unique opportunity to accelerate our growth. The more we confront ourselves, the more we are inspired. The speedier our development through the accumulation of experience the more frequent our incarnations.

A soul that hasn't had many incarnations will have different standards of morality than a soul which has been here often. In early incarnations, a soul will be completely given over to physical appetites. Eventually, this type of soul must confront itself and its surrounding world. Self-contemplation leads to higher morality, a refinement and purification of self—and the development of a more spiritual life. Subsequently, in successive incarnations, sensory desire alone will no longer be the criteria of our sojourn; morality begins to purify the animal instincts. With each life, the individual's moral code and aspirations are raised, as it continually directs itself toward perfection.

Food, sex, alcohol, and other sensual appetites are nonexistent in the spirit-world. Therefore you can only practice refining, attuning, and balancing these aspects of yourself here on Earth, where these expressions afford you opportunities for working out karma and gaining equilibrium.

Each child has actually chosen its characteristics and talents. The more advanced the soul, the more carefully it selects the appropriate conditions to be born into. It's not only the child's selection; the parent selects the child for similar purposes. The choice is reciprocal and is mutually conceived in the spirit-world. Being who you are, you attract the very souls with whom you have been involved before. They, too, need similar conditions in which to grow. Wherever close relationships are concerned, especially between parents and children, husbands and wives, these souls have met many times before. This is part of a plan originating in the spirit-world where a specific mutual incarnation is necessary.

Time does not exist in the spirit-world. Parents and children contemplate their next incarnation simultaneously without regard for the chronology of earth time. These forthcoming involvements are prepared for in timelessness.

Often we select parents with ideas and traits seemingly dissimilar to our own precisely because it affords us an added opportunity to adjust to them in developing an harmonious life. Instead of rejecting such situations as irritating polarities, or moving away from them as though they didn't exist, embracing and accepting these challenges speeds up our unfolding toward enlightenment, and our personal gain is made all the more manifest.

To lose a child is one of the most tragic experiences a person can select. This could well be the result of the parent having committed suicide in a previous incarnation. Karma always balances out. A woman who abandons her children in one life may experience the loss of a child in a subsequent life. A man who abandons his family may return as a woman unable to bear children.

Thousands of people have experienced devastating earthquakes. They have seen the earth open up and swallow their children and loved ones in front of their eyes and then succumbed themselves. The underlying subconscious memory of this horrifying scene, the inconsolable loss, causes fear of giving birth in subsequent lives, fear of experiencing loss all over again. It creates the ambivalence of wanting a child and looking ahead to the moment of birth with trepidation. This is one reason certain women suffer great pain in childbirth.

In the Bible it is said that Jesus healed a man who had been blind from birth. His disciples asked him who had erred, the man or his parents, for the man surely couldn't have sinned before he was born. Their question contains the whole revelation of the reincarnational cycle: How *could* he have sinned before birth unless he had previously lived and come into his present life to make up the balance? A similar concept is put forth in the Old Testament: "An eye for an eye, and a tooth for a tooth." This is not simply a call to revenge present injustices. It refers to settling accounts in a reincarnational sense. As you have sown in previous lives, so you will reap in this or future lives.

Sometimes a soul will come into an incarnation too quickly, not selecting carefully enough, and will find that this particular life cannot fulfill or advance its consciousness. The soul then chooses to cut life short. "Accidents," death at birth, infancy, or early childhood may very well be indications of this. The soul returns to its spirit-state to better prepare for the proper conditions in terms of its karmic indebtedness.

What we must always remember is that karma can be erased, the slate can be wiped clean. The choice is always yours. And you can start right now. Every action, every thought, every deed, every experience we've ever had, past and present, is indelibly recorded for every one of us. We carry this sum total at all times. This is why potentially we are so phenomenal.

Karma means you must *pay up now*. You can't put off, procrastinate, or postpone. You must pay up now, because your growth, your person, your very soul is at stake. This is the only purpose of your being here on Earth.

It is not God who sits in judgment of us, who decrees who shall be singled out or punished. Nor does God decide the time of death for anyone. It is your own consciousness and your own activity which determines your life. You judge yourself. You must be prepared to pay your debts and meet your karma.

Erasing Karma

Prior to our birth into this dimension, we are already conditioned to perceive the realities of this planet. We are ready to grasp our Earth experiences with great intensity when we let everything talk to us from an inner process of feelings.

If we would accept reincarnation and its laws as governing our personal experiences, we would change much more rapidly. Our personal conduct, attitudes, and actions would alter our lives dramatically. We would offer our services to others. Living by these laws accentuate our purpose and give meaning to our lives.

By committing a wrong (toward another or toward ourselves), we accumulate debts. This karma carries its own consequences—either in this life span or another. Realizing this should motivate us in our every activity, pointing the way to a better, more profound life, a true moral existence.

True morality, perfection of self, and assuming full responsibility for ourselves would generate a love that would come to prevent war, violence, and prejudice. By understanding life on a large scale, the contribution of each individual would become vital and have an enduring consequence for the future.

We meet ourselves coming and going, whether here on Earth in a physical body, in the spirit dimension in the shape appropriate to our consciousness, or in the dream reality when we are asleep. We might choose not to look at it, but it's true, nevertheless: Everything you encounter is you; everything is a reflection of you.

The fastest way to erase karma, indeed the only way to wipe it out, is through love, kindness, and understanding—to yourself, to people in need, to anything and everything. Deep love must be your only motivation.

Your free will is dependent on your intelligent choices. You are not restricted to karma, you can eliminate it. And there is no time limit. It can go at a fantastic speed if you choose to live life with love and reverence. You can start immediately, at this very moment. It will forever change the course of events in your world.

CHAPTER NINE

A TRIP TO BADGASTEIN

Fear is the antithesis of love.
Profound love dispels all fear.

KARMA REVISITED

One wintry Saturday afternoon in 1973, I attended a Broadway matinee in New York City with a friend. Coming out of the theater after the performance, we saw that it had begun to pour. We were only two of hundreds of people standing under the marquee hoping for a cab to come along. Faced with the possibility of remaining there for hours or getting drenched, my friend suddenly remembered a nearby restaurant where she knew the manager, a man named Leo. I vaguely recalled meeting him. He was an old friend of hers and she knew he would be happy to see us. We decided it would be better to sit out the weather over a drink or two, so we scurried under awnings, from doorway to doorway, until we found the place.

As he greeted and showed us to a table, I was amazed by his appearance. I had met Leo only once before, a few years earlier, and remembered him as looking much older. Now lines had disappeared from his face, there was a spring in his step, and his eyes sparkled with enthusiasm. He was a new man, in the true sense of the word. After we had relaxed and talked a bit, I was unable to contain myself any longer. "What have you been doing with yourself?" I inquired. "You look twenty years younger."

He beamed as he described a spa he had visited twice in Austria, near Salzburg, a place called Badgastein. Located high in the mountains, amid breathtaking waterfalls, it was reputed to be a "fountain of youth." Natural thermal pools and mineral springs had made it a Mecca for people seeking to restore their health. He spoke glowingly of the programs there and offered to send me some literature about the area which he had at home.

I had become so enthusiastic about the place merely by seeing him that I decided right away to tell my father, who had been looking for exactly this kind of health cure. When I got home that night, I called Papa and he became so excited that he said, "We'll all go! I'll take you and the girls with me."

Two weeks went by, and I heard nothing from Leo. I called him and he apologized, saying he hadn't been able to find the folders. I decided to go directly to a travel agency and let them handle the arrangements. Although it was a large agency, they had never heard of Badgastein. I had to press them to write to the Austrian tourist bureau for information. After a lengthy, complicated correspondence, we finally had a reservation on a flight for Salzburg.

Looking over various brochures, I felt drawn to a hotel located on top of one of the mountains in the area, with (as the folder described) beautiful views, clear mountain air, and a complete treatment program in their own thermal pools. But at the last moment we decided to economize and settled for a much smaller place, the Pension Hildebrandt, situated in the valley. We would have to travel back and forth from the public pools to our lodgings but that didn't seem such a hardship in view of the money we would save. We made a reservation for a suite in the pension with all meals included.

The first leg of our flight took us to Zurich. My father loves good food but the food on the plane was awful. We arrived on a blisteringly hot summer day and had to sit in the airport for two hours to make the Salzburg connection. Famished, we boarded the second plane for the half-hour flight.

In Salzburg, we discovered that the travel agent had totally misinformed us about the schedule. We had been told a train was to leave for Badgastein just as we arrived. There was none. Instead, there was a bus, but it only ran once a day, and we had missed it by two hours. Exhausted, barely able to hold up in the heat, we decided to take a taxi, thinking it would be cheaper than spending the night at a hotel. It wasn't. The drive took over three hours and the fare was astronomical.

All of these difficulties should have alerted me that the trip was ill-fated. I was moving against the stream. When so many obstacles and inconveniences are placed in your path, they signal you that perhaps you should not go on. Continuing against your better judgment indicates a strong force at work, karma.

By this time the children were irritable and the heat unbearable. On top of that, the driver didn't know his way around the small, out-of-the-way valley, and we had to stop several times to get directions from passersby. When he finally said, "I think that's the place up ahead," I could hardly believe it. I felt an odd sensation in the pit of my stomach. My first instinctive reaction was to say, "Take us elsewhere." But Papa and the girls were so relieved to get out of the cab and stretch that I dismissed my uneasiness.

The Pension Hildebrandt was obviously old, done in a chalet-type style. Solid brown timbers framed dark stucco walls with little gingerbread trimmings around the roof and windows. It was a four-story structure set in a tiny town that belonged on a picture postcard. Surrounded by mountains and waterfalls on all sides, the little village of Badgastein had

ignored the passage of time. The people in the narrow streets
and their way of life looked as if they had remained un-
changed for hundreds of years. As we walked into the
entryway of the pension a woman who introduced herself as
Fraulein Inge appeared. She greeted us and insisted on carrying all our suitcases upstairs. She explained that Frau Lisl, the
owner and manager, was away and would return later that
evening.

When she opened the door to our suite on the second
floor, we saw a long, windowless hall lined with built-in cup-
boards and closets. The first door on the right was the bathroom, and I was surprised to see that everything throughout
the interior of the place was modern and up to date. It was
anachronous compared to the rustic, colorless appearance
of the exterior and the quaint town we had just driven
through. Next, on the right, was a door to a bedroom, facing
a tiled courtyard, where Papa and Luana were to sleep. And
last, on the left at the far end of the hall, was a bed-sitting
room where Adina and I would stay.

I went to the large bay window of our room, opened the
heavy flowered drapes, and saw that the window looked out
over the street below. Directly opposite was another gingerbread house where a round-faced man sat in a chair at his
own window. He seemed like a piece of furniture himself as
he stared blankly across at me, never moving.

Papa and the girls immediately fell asleep on their beds,
but I was unable to shrug off my forebodings about the
place. I busied myself unpacking. A few hours later I woke
them to go downstairs for dinner. The dining room was
filled with guests, mostly Germans. Reservations were
checked and we discovered we had not been expected for
dinner or any meal, for that matter. Grudgingly, Fraulein
Inge managed to scrape up something for us to eat. The food
was terrible.

Later that evening, Frau Lisl returned and came upstairs
to welcome us. A tall, handsome woman, she exuded effi-

ciency and authority. Graciously, she arranged for our medical appointments the next day. I had decided to take the cure with Papa, and a doctor's certification of health was mandatory before beginning the rigorous schedule of hot mineral baths. Frau Lisl offered to drive us to the doctor herself, but there was something about her that didn't sit right with me.

I was born in Germany, but we had left when I was eight and I never had the desire to go back. We had not been directly affected by any of the things that took place under the Third Reich, but I have never been able to erase my knowledge of the holocaust. Among Frau Lisl's guests was Herr Erhart, a Berliner who visited Badgastein every year. He and I got to know one another, talking often about Germany and Austria, how they had changed since the war and how they had not.

One afternoon as Herr Erhart and I sat talking in the dining room over cups of coffee, watching the rain batter against the windows, I noticed three strange men come into the lobby. They wore high leather boots and even clicked their heels when they addressed anyone. Their behavior was cool and abrupt, they had no manners at all, and they expected everything to be done for them. Frau Lisl catered to them completely, addressing them by their first names. It was obvious that they were policemen or officials of some sort, and yet they made themselves perfectly at home, as if they owned the place.

Sensing my uneasiness, Herr Erhart wanted to reassure me that he was not one of them. He was a universal person, he said, but he warned me, nevertheless. "Don't be fooled by appearances," he said. "Behind the facade, Nazism is still very much alive. In Berlin it's out in the open. Hatred of Jews still prevails. Don't think anything has changed."

As the days went by, my father began to dwell on his past, the war, the Germans, Hitler, our escape, his memories of the things that had caused us to leave Germany. I assumed that Hitler's influence had not reached this remote valley, since we had seen many Hassidic Jewish tourists in the vicinity. A beautiful young woman, Frau Boehm, came in to clean our rooms each day. She was a lovely person who had lived in the valley all her life, and we became friends right away. One day I decided to ask her what was on my mind. "What was it like here during the war under Hitler?"

At the risk of her job, in whispered tones, she began to describe what she remembered. As a young girl during the war, her large family lived off the land. There had been a kindly Jewish doctor in the village who had cared for them when they were sick. Being poor, they worried about not being able to pay him, but he would always smile and say, "Don't worry about it. Someday, if you have the money, you can pay me." They cherished this man. But one day he disappeared and was never heard of again. Rumor had it that he'd been taken to a concentration camp in Poland. Frau Boehm began to cry. She had not erased the memory in over thirty years.

I began to look forward to her daily visits. The more we talked, the more I learned about Badgastein during the war. She told me that Frau Lisl had housed important Nazi officials at the pension and in return for her services, the Nazis arranged to have the entire place modernized at no cost to her. Frau Lisl had participated in everything that occurred in the valley, particularly the atrocities toward Jews. In the middle of the night, old and young were bodily loaded on to trucks and shipped off to destinations unknown; they were never to return. Frau Boehm recounted more unpleasant details, but the most startling was that Hitler himself had come to Badgastein every year to take the cure and had stayed at Frau Lisl's pension!

I began to remember that Austria had been as fanatical as Germany in persecuting Jews. Salzburg and Badgastein were in fact central train connections from which hundreds of thousands of Jews were sent to their deaths. Now that I had heard about Frau Lisl and her involvement with these horrors, our stay at the pension became intolerable. But there was more in store.

A couple of weeks after our arrival, the dollar declined and the rate of exchange shifted. I asked Frau Lisl to estimate what our bill would be in shillings by the time we left three weeks hence. Her demeanor changed as abruptly as the monetary rate. She was infuriated by my request and subsequently presented me with a staggering bill for the brief time we had already been there. Every cup of coffee was a dollar, every little thing was charged as an extra, although our original understanding was that it was all-inclusive in the price of our rooms. At this point, Papa and I decided we would take our meals elsewhere, since the food was so awful anyway.

The heat when we arrived had been oppressive, and the abnormally high temperatures continued for the first few days we were there. Then it began to rain in torrents without letup, and we never saw the sun again for the rest of our stay. By now, Frau Lisl had changed from a gracious, considerate hostess to a rude tyrant who wanted nothing to do with us. Each time we passed her in the lobby, she glared. The atmosphere was charged.

Luana and Adina had little to do; there were no programmed activities for children. The local color in the village consisted of three events. Every afternoon at four o'clock three cows were brought in from the fields and herded down the street in front of the pension with their bells clanking, which was the signal for the little round-faced man across from our window to go downstairs, pick up his newspaper, and have a stein of beer. By 4:15, he was back at his post, staring at us from across the way. Every morning, at precisely ten o'clock, two old ladies dressed entirely in black would meet under our window to exchange gossip: one did all the talking, the other listened and nodded.

The children grew rowdy and bored, and my father now demanded constant attention. He was forever discussing his war memories and became increasingly impatient with the girls. I became the mediator, trying to keep peace.

Then the nightmares began.

Each night, when I finally got to sleep, I had the same nightmare: The number "1668" flashed repeatedly in front of my eyes. Far underground, in a damp, cold dungeon, I was locked in a room with a man. Everything was in darkness. From beyond the heavy, bolted door came anguished cries of tortured souls. People were facing pain and death in the next room. The man and I knew that we must do something, that it was only a matter of minutes before we would be brought into that other room, but he was afraid that we would be killed. I whispered that we would be killed anyway, that we would have to put a stop to the atrocities going on in there. Across the room was a strange, ancient switch of some sort. It was the only thing in the dream that was white, that could be seen clearly. I knew somehow that if I could get across the room without being noticed and throw that switch, it would help in some way. But I never did anything.

Night after night, I suffered through this same scene. At first I would never get across the room, but in time I finally would attempt to throw the switch, knowing that it would save lives. At last, I would reach for the switch and a hand out of the darkness would grab my wrist. Horrified, I would see that it was my father. "Don't do it," he would say. Shaking with fear, I would wake up screaming. After each nightmare, I found my right hand actually swollen, accompanied by excruciating pain, which took hours to subside.

Luana was having nightmares, too, but at first was overwrought and reluctant to tell me. I eventually got her to describe them: She was in a dungeon, standing in front of a strange tribunal. Robed figures were questioning her. Torture instruments lined the room and there was blood everywhere. She knew she was going to die, and she was terrified. They used a strange device to cut off her arm. At the point of

seeing her arm dangling in the dream, she too would wake
up screaming uncontrollably.

Adina and Luana switched rooms, so that Luana and I
could be together. We were both afraid to go to sleep. We
would stay up as late as possible, playing all sorts of card
games, but eventually we would grow weary and fall asleep,
and the terrifying nightmares would start up again. My father had been having nightmares as well. From the few de-
scriptions I could drag out of him, it turned out that his
dreams took place in exactly the same dungeon and involved the same horrible circumstances.

Our days grew more and more miserable, our nights
even worse. We all felt trapped. The pension became a
prison. My father was constantly snapping at Luana, telling
her she couldn't do anything right. Between trying to constantly smooth things over, the nightmares, and everything
else, my nerves were frayed to the breaking point.

One morning I was awakened by thunderous knocking
at our door. Fraulein Inge came storming in like a mad-
woman, yelling hysterically about a broken cup. She accused
me of having smashed the cup and thrown it into the courtyard. I immediately thought of the children. I didn't know
what she was talking about, but I knew I didn't like her manner, which was arrogant and abusive. After Fraulein Inge left,
slamming the door behind her, I confronted the girls: What
did they know about a cup? I knew from the start that Luana
had something to do with it because she was sitting not
making a sound. I didn't want to direct my words solely at
her, so I gave both girls an hour to think about it.

Five minutes later Luana came to me in tears and explained what had happened. Wanting a drink of water, she
had gone to the cupboard and removed a cup. She was so
nervous since Papa had begun criticizing her every move
that she had dropped the cup and broken it. Afraid to tell
anyone and thinking that the scene would be unbearable,

she wrapped the cup in toilet paper and threw it out the window into the courtyard when no one was looking. I reassured her that we would get everything straightened out and pay for the precious cup.

By now I was fed up. Determined to settle things once and for all, I went downstairs. I told Frau Lisl that I had never encountered such behavior. "What right," I said, "did Fraulein Inge have to yell at a guest about something as insignificant as a cup?" Frau Lisl icily informed me that Fraulein Inge was her partner, not merely an employee, and as such she totally approved of her actions. She went on to demand a ridiculous price for what I learned was a common stoneware cup. Thoroughly intimidated, I paid her the money and went back upstairs, shaking. Her attitude had been defiant and ugly. I felt she had treated me like a Nazi would treat a Jew.

I hadn't been upstairs five minutes when the door opened and Adina flew into the room crying. The imprint of five fingers was scarlet on her cheek. She said Fraulein Inge had slapped her and called her a dirty Jew. Stunned, I stood motionless. My worst fears had been confirmed. I could take no more. I had reached the breaking point. I went to my father and pleaded that we leave the pension immediately and move elsewhere. He resisted, arguing that it was impossible to disrupt the schedule of the cure, and that we would be leaving in less than a week anyway. Exhausted, I gave in.

That night, after waking up screaming again from the same nightmare, I had to go to the bathroom. There was no light in the hall, and not wanting to awaken anyone, I slipped out of my room and began to walk down the long corridor in the dark. Suddenly, just outside Papa's room, I sensed a figure on my left. A man, dressed in tatters, reached toward me with his hand. I ran past him into the bathroom, slammed the door, and turned on the light. My heart was pounding. Had I actually seen a figure, or was I losing my mind?

Trembling, I peeked down the hall and saw him still standing there. I was so terrified that I ran past him back to my room, not daring to look. The incident was so upsetting, I decided not to mention it to the others. I wasn't sure of anything anymore. From then on I left the light on in the bathroom.

The following night Luana had another of her nightmares. Her crying awakened me. "I have to go to the bathroom, Mommy," she said. Not wanting to put anything into her mind and not wanting to frighten her, I waited inside our room as she started down the corridor. I heard her gasp and my heart sank. I knew she had seen what I had seen. I went out into the hall in front of our door and saw her standing at the other end, frozen with fear, not knowing what to do. I shouted to her, "Don't look at it. Just run to me." She closed her eyes and ran into my arms. Sitting on our bed, we tried to calm one another. I began to pray that we wouldn't have to go through that hallway ever again at night.

But the more I considered the figure we had seen, the less frightened I became. He was not threatening. He was pitiful, pleading for help, beckoning to me with his outstretched hand. It suddenly occurred to me that this was the same theme of my nightmares: a cry for help, for rescue. But I felt I couldn't help him or anyone, including myself. I too was a prisoner in that place and just as helpless.

A few days before we were to leave, who should appear but Leo, the restaurant manager from New York. By accident, we had picked the very hotel where he always stayed. I was relieved to see him. In a rush of excitement, I began to describe what had gone on at the pension during the war. I left out no detail of what Frau Boehm had told me regarding the abominations committed by Frau Lisl. As I talked, Leo kept looking away and changing the subject. Members of his very own family had died in concentration camps, but he didn't wish to hear what I had to say.

At long last the day of departure arrived. We struggled down the stairs with our baggage, all thirteen pieces. By this time we were so totally ostracized, no one would help us. As we stood in the lobby, impatiently waiting for our taxi, Frau Lisl's father appeared. He was a remarkable man, in a world all his own, a symbol of youth at eighty-seven. His conversation had always been pleasant and gentle. He suddenly said to me, "I never showed you our wine cellar, did I? It's the only part of the house that dates back hundreds of years. Everything else has been rebuilt. Come, let me show it to you."

Before I could decline, he took me by the hand and led Luana and me to a door near the back of the lobby. When he unlocked it, it sprung wide open, and a cold draft overwhelmed us. Descending the twisting stone stairs, I couldn't believe what my eyes beheld. It was the very dungeon of my nightmares! Luana also recognized it at once. We held onto one another, shivering and exchanging glances of horror, wanting only to get away from that miserable place and its memories. We practically tripped over each other in our wild haste to flee. When we got upstairs and out into the street, the sun literally burst through the clouds. It—and we—had finally emerged after five weeks of bleakness, imprisonment, and despair.

It was late afternoon when the driver loaded our luggage into the taxi. Getting in, I looked up for the last time and caught a glimpse of the round-faced man sitting in his window across the street. The only difference now was that he raised his arm to wave good-bye to us. I had never been more relieved than when, at last, we drove away from the quaint, picturesque valley of Badgastein.

When we arrived back home in America, I went into isolation. For months I wouldn't see clients or friends. I was haunted by this trip. I didn't know what to make of it. I couldn't connect.

I went to see a medium. The first thing she told me was that I had had an incarnation in the mountains of Austria in the seventeenth century. A chill ran through me. She lowered her voice. "Your life then came to an abrupt end by being pushed off a cliff into a waterfall as part of some religious persecution." It was then that I told her of the misery of my recent trip. She immediately said, "You had no business being there in 1973." I could not accept that. The fact that I had re-experienced this trauma told me there was something that connected with my life today.

I had to ask myself, "Why did I stick it out? Why did I remain in the pension knowing full well what was going on?" It was as if I was hypnotized, frozen to the spot, a frightened, helpless child. That was the key: helplessness and overwhelming fear. In all my nightmares, I had not been able to rescue myself or others in desperate need. So too in my daily experiences at Badgastein, I could not find the courage to act. I was afraid, in spite of my convictions. I had felt all along that I should report what I had learned about Frau Lisl's activities to the authorities, but I was scared to death we would be locked up on some pretense and never be heard from again. Frau Lisl and her friends had been involved in untold atrocities, and their cruelty, arrogance, and prejudice was still apparent. I should have done something, at the very least left the pension, but I didn't—out of fear, cowardice, and as I learned later, karma. There was a lesson to be learned at Badgastein and once again I was the student.

We are never rid of anything unless it is lovingly resolved. As I come to a larger understanding of the karma of Badgastein, I am freer of it. Cowardice and fear would have to be overcome. The challenges and difficulties will always be there, until they are met. There is but one tool to master such a task: Love. Love under the most adverse circumstances, in everything, *for all*, including the Lisls and Inges of the world. Indeed, profound love dispels all fear.

CHAPTER TEN

WHERE ARE YOU GOING?

Love is the sole reason for our existence.
If love does not determine our every action,
we have lost a life span.

ASTROLOGY

The way astrology is practiced today is totally different from
the way it was conceived thousands of years ago. Today
charts are cast from the time of birth, which is not the critical point of an individual's beginning at all. The point of
conception is actually more revealing, yet there are other
influences of even greater impact to consider. As a result,
most astrological predictions and interpretations are subject
to inaccuracy, not only by nine months (from the point of
conception), but for lack of consideration for the time
the soul has traveled to conception, to its entrance into life
on Earth. Where has the soul been prior to this life? What
planets have influenced, fortified and prepared it for this
sojourn?

To gain insight into where a soul has traveled previous to
its incarnation here would require a combination astrologer-
psychic medium with clairvisual, clairvoyant, clairaudient
abilities. This person would have to have an extremely high

consciousness to perceive where a soul has traveled, in order to draw up a really accurate chart. This was the way it was practiced in Babylonian times.

As commonly practiced today, astrology is subject to even further error: as yet, not every sign of the zodiac has its corresponding planet. There are planets in our solar system scientists will one day discover. All twelve are not yet known.

Although astrology today is pretty much of a parlor game, there is some merit to it. Supposedly, if you're born under a certain sign, you exhibit certain traits. In the broadest sense this is true, because there are indeed only twelve types. We are born under a particular sign for specific reasons. Within each sign there are challenges to be worked out. However, by simply accepting the tendencies, and limiting yourself to characteristic signs, you fall into a trap of limitation. Signs do not dictate—you do. We can do something about everything in our life.

To use astrology correctly take it from the premise of its challenges. Each sign has negative aspects which alert you to your task. If you accept and meet these challenges, in order to work on and perfect yourself, then astrology has a great deal to offer. For example, if you are born a Capricorn, your chief negative trait is stubbornness. Therefore, you are called upon to become more flexible and open-minded. If your sign is Leo, overcoming selfishness is your primary challenge. Learn to show consideration and love for your fellow human beings. Eventually, through each sign, the perfected individual is the one who has worked out the negativities of the entire zodiac. We are not dominated by one sign alone. Other planetary forces intermingle within our sign. If you met a hundred Libras, each born on the same day, you'd still meet a hundred different individuals. They may bear similarities of character, yet each must work out consciousness on an individual basis.

To guard against the weaknesses of your sign, aim for its

opposite. This is the work you have chosen to do in this life to achieve balance. Nothing is permanently fixed. Even lines in your palm change, based on self-improvement and accomplishment. Likewise, readings change based on your efforts and degree of self-growth. Palmistry, readings, astrology—these are *corresponding* forces, not *causal* ones. You can build your life around an astrological sign if you choose and make endless excuses about forces beyond your control. There is nothing noble in this. Chances are you are stuck and merely trying to justify your situation. More excitingly, you can select the perfecting of self under the challenges and difficulties your sign denotes.

Never limit yourself to a sign or symbol. You can surpass all.

YOUR DESTINY NUMBER

An added source of information to further self-exploration is numerology. There is mathematical order to the entire universe and numbers are a direct link. An example of numerology that you can apply immediately to yourself is your destiny number.

Working with names can be complicated (you're born with one name, you may acquire a nickname, and you can change your name legally or through marriage). Therefore, your destiny number, which you carry throughout life, is simpler to figure out. It is yet another means of zeroing in on the weaker traits you have chosen to work out here on Earth.

Write down your date of birth: month, date, and year. Add the digits in each figure consecutively until they are reduced to one digit. For example, suppose you were born on September 28, 1944. The *month* is 9. The *date* is 2+8, or 10, which is reduced to 1. The *year* is $1 + 9 + 4 + 4$, or 18, which is reduced to 9. The remaining three figures are $9 + 1 + 9$.

Now add these together and reduce them to one digit. $9 + 1 + 9 = 19$; $1 + 9 = 10$, and $1 + 0 = 1$. (With 10, zero comes into play, emphasizing the 1, giving it more meaning than if it stood alone. The same emphasis would apply if the number were 20, 30, or 40.)

What applies to astrology also applies to numerology. From a consciousness point of view, the significant traits are the weaker ones, which give an indication of the work you must do on yourself. Each number carries its own vibration:

1 **is solitary**, single-minded, a loner. Someone who has got to do things by himself or herself, without help from anyone else. The challenge here is to learn to cooperate, get along with others, and to include the world.

2 **is duality**. This person is in conflict with everything. The tendency is to vacillate between choices, often getting stuck through indecision. The challenge here is to harmonize within self to unify conscious and subconscious mind.

3 **is a powerful number**, calling for unification of the three minds. Harmony within self on all three levels— conscious, subconscious, and superconscious—is the task here. Without this inner togetherness, advancement is impossible, resulting in much turmoil throughout life.

4 **is patience and practicality**. This person is consumed by details and worries about the outcome of everything. Challenge: to relax, let go. To expand, probe, and explore the inner being; to curtail extravagance and be more practical in dealing with life's daily tasks, especially in spending money.

5 **is change**, an impulsive person. An adventure-seeker. This individual must carefully and deliberately direct his or her path in life. A high purpose, not merely an escape, must be the inspiration for advancement.

6 **is teaching**, imparting knowledge. These persons share,

give of themselves, but are inclined to procrastinate and let others carry the load. They exemplify their beliefs, particularly spiritual knowledge. When their voice becomes their instrument, they will practice what they preach.

7 **is spirituality**. Not everyone with a seven is necessarily leading a spiritual life, however. They may be intuitively probing themselves, but tend to get caught up in the material world. Unless they lead their life from their feeling center, they will have a difficult time finding themselves.

8 **is success**. Money and the good life come all too easily to these persons. Therefore, their challenge is not to put too much emphasis on material things (even though material success, too, is a level of consciousness), but to include the inner spiritual world in their life.

9 **is challenge** to serve humanity. These persons give of themselves. It completes the cycle of numbers, and consequently such people need to get rid of the old, and start anew, whether spiritually or materially. Generosity and charity must be accentuated, toward others and oneself.

There are three *master numbers*. They can be reduced further, but the potential within the master number should be considered. The vibration here is extremely high.

11 **is execution**. The challenge is to put into action whatever qualities and talent are evident in the individual. This pertains to any area of life—material, artistic, and spiritual. A typical *11* tends to be impractical—the artist lost in artistry, not in touch with the reality of one's surroundings. The potential for execution is there, once the balance within is found. Eleven also reduces to 2, and here is where one is alerted to be careful. *Two* is duality, cross-purpose. Unification here is important in order to best serve the purpose of this master number. So, too, is selflessness because the two *1*'s imply egotistic leanings.

22 is accomplishment in artistry, show-business, designing, painting, performing, any creative endeavor. Such persons can apply their talents. But *22* reduces to *4*, and the task here is to remain centered in a practical way. Four also contains two *2*'s—a double duality. The challenge here is to point creative energies in one direction, yet remain practical.

33 is the highest master number, signifying spiritual realization. The challenge is to share and impart to the world, by example. Jesus vibrated to *33*. Involved here are two *3*'s—double unification of the conscious, subconscious, and superconscious mind. Reduced to *6*, it calls for the giving and teaching of spiritual knowledge through personal wisdom and love.

Nothing is accidental. Your birth was very well designed, through your own master planning. In your essence-state of being you have contemplated yourself very carefully, without distraction. You have selected the very year, month, day, and many other details of your life, large and small, to better work out what you need to balance, advance, and complete your evolvement based on the deeds and experiences of your past lives.

You cannot ignore your own selections. You have made your choices in order to overcome karmically the difficulties now encountered. In so doing you supersede all, eliminating your karmic debt. By erasing karma now, it will not be necessary for you to carry these debts into subsequent lives. You'll have freed yourself. This knowledge gives you the opportunity to understand that you can and must tackle everything!

Though you may have selected only a part of your work for this particular incarnation, through these insights you can now include things you did not prepare yourself for in your essence-state. Do not allow yourself to be passively reduced to a number, zodiac sign, or even a lifetime of heavy karma. You can open your channels to work out everything—even things you haven't imagined or thought of yet.

DIVORCE AND KARMA

Often people who are seriously probing and working on themselves will ask if their karmic debt is also the karmic debt of their spouse. In other words, does divorce cut off an opportunity for a couple to work out their karma with each other?

The case of a woman I know may serve as an example. Seriously wanting to work out all her karmic debts, she realized she couldn't work them out with her ex-husband any longer. He was out of her life. She was troubled by the thought that the opportunity was no longer available, and that this karma would remain hanging over her unresolved. What could she do now?

After many long hours of contemplation, she arrived at the conclusion that her karma with this man was over. However, if there were any remaining karmic factors for her to deal with, they would present themselves within a similar relationship with another man. *The opportunities are endless, constantly available to us, even though they may seem to be cut off.* When you can't do anything about a given situation, you have to accept it as the best thing that ever happened to you. Where two souls are involved, it takes a common contribution to work out karma together. When this is no longer possible, it comes down to one's own individual karma, which is never limited in its opportunities. If it is not resolved in the first act by one set of characters, the second act of the karmic drama will unfold with an entirely new cast.

Childless marriages ending in divorce clearly have a lesser karmic connection than marriages with children.

More often than not, the wife carries the heavier burden when her mate leaves. A wife tends to get stuck equating through the mind of her husband, whether he left her for another woman or not. "How could he abandon his home, his very own child?" she asks. It would seem inconceivable to give up the involvement, joy, and opportunity that goes along with parenting, watching the child's development, guiding it into maturity with true purpose. Nevertheless, it does not help to equate in this way. Quite the contrary, hurt and recrimination set negative attitudes in motion for the abandoned mate and postpone personal growth. Obviously if the abandoning mate's consciousness were ready for the parent role, no difficulty would be great enough to make him (or her) relinquish the responsibility.

Blaming another never helps. Anger is self-defeating. Be your own equation. See the marvelous opportunity you now have as a mother or a father. Your challenge becomes two-fold: It puts you in the marvelous position of being both parents at once. Thus your own consciousness and awareness are heightened more rapidly. Your own development is tested. Child-rearing should never be considered a chore. By welcoming your challenge as a wonderful opportunity, abundant love will dominate in guiding your children. In retrospect, you will see it as one of the most valuable and gratifying experiences of your life. Instead of hatred and resentment, you will give thanks to the one who left you.

In addition, you must realize that your children in their essence-state have also determined this destiny through their own selection. They have played as big a part as you have in creating the situation. In the spirit-world, between death and a new birth, they determined that at some point they would have no further need for a particular parent.

What they had to work out no longer included a father, a mother, or sometimes both. It is clear that the karmic relationship pertains directly to the parent primarily responsible for the children. We have predetermined and chosen the very circumstance we find ourselves in. You must not forget that.

Right now, in this country, divorce is sky-rocketing, obviously a matter of group karma. It's still not happening as carelessly elsewhere in the world as it is here at home, where both marriage and divorce are entered into frivolously. As individuals, however, American or otherwise, we can remove ourselves from this or any group karma through larger understanding and greater effort.

All marriages can work, when both parties are desirous. But they must deliberately and consciously apply themselves to the task. We need to consider marriage more seriously, more wantingly, *more sacredly* rather than moving from one relationship to another without giving the existing union a chance to grow. We tend to look for external influences to inspire us, when in fact we need to, and can only, inspire ourselves from within for love to endure. Our own inner resources are the never-ending forces of life.

Beginnings are always exciting, particularly in personal relationships. Why? Because in wanting to be loved and accepted, we give freely of ourselves, without putting demands on the other person. The question is: How do we sustain the newness of love? The answer is simple but the application more difficult. We must treat every moment of a relationship as the beginning. Never take another person for granted. We must always see him or her through new eyes.

SEX AND MORALITY

Morality, as exercised today, is constantly changing as society changes in accordance with its own karma and convenience. But there is a higher morality, a morality born of the spiritual mind. It has encompassing love at its center, and service to humanity as its purpose. Here on Earth, where distractions are continual, it is easy to mislead oneself into a false sense of morality, by registering experiences solely through the five senses. Sensory distractions and immorality dim our perception of our true purpose on this planet.

The sexual experience is a strong one, be it for pleasure

or procreation. Mingled with sensation, it makes us feel alive—if only temporarily. Too often, however, it is abused, serving to divert and distract us from our true mission in life. Much too readily we succumb to our sexual appetites, often losing our balance and identity along the way. Promiscuity is rampant. Sex has become love's replacement, yet the hunger for real love persists and that is why the search continues.

Society cannot set the standard for your moral code. You must discern it for yourself. You must feel for yourself. You can't allow any authority to dictate what is right or wrong. Only by summoning all your inner strength and by probing deeply, will you find the answers you seek. The answers never come from out there. They come from deep within you. The soul is the moral gauge.

Nothing is clear from the point of view of a single life-time, but everything comes together in terms of many lives. Any sort of deviation in sexual behavior can be better understood reincarnationally. Homosexuality, for instance, is usually the result of a sudden change to the opposite gender. Such a soul has spent several consecutive lives as one sex and then found the need to move to the opposite sex. The changeover is often so abrupt that some souls find it difficult to adjust to their new gender. Homosexuals still crave the sexual partner familiar to them from past incarnations.

In the case of a male homosexual, in all likelihood his past several lives were experienced as a woman. He carries with him certain female traits not previously worked out, and these further color his degree of femininity. The soul dons a man's body, but finds the subconscious memory of the woman's role more decisive. It is a direct carryover from past life experiences and this soul is not making the proper adjustment to the male role selected. The same thing applies to a woman leaning toward homosexuality. Lesbians act on their subconscious memories of having been men in previous consecutive lives.

Homosexuality is dealt with today in terms of only the

current life. Therapists talk of domineering mothers for men, or domineering fathers in the case of women. Yet these very attractions were considered by the soul before coming into a particular family. These are the exact challenges the soul has selected to work out. Parents do play a valid role. But sexual preference has its beginnings in a different dimension.

Once homosexuals understand this, the challenges they face become exciting invitations to self-enlightenment. Acceptance of the body we were born with is the message of truth of who we really are. It is we who have chosen the body our soul dwells in. Therefore, we must fulfill the role we are destined to play. Spiritual growth is dependent on the change of gender from one incarnation to the next. The energies that govern and sustain the existence of life on planet Earth are the polarities of male and female. These nurturing energies propagate our species and bring forth the next generation of beings waiting in the wings of the spirit realm, ready to descend to earthly incarnation. Anything that hinders this creative process is an interference with life on this planet and our true human purpose.

Today homosexuals have become—like almost every other group—militant and outspoken. And therein lies the danger. Group thinking will not solve individual problems. One must look at oneself as a spiritual entity and realize that one's own individual conscience is the most perfect teacher. Ancient Greece is often evoked as a cultural excuse for today's homosexual lifestyle. What has been forgotten is that it was group karma then as it is now, and sooner or later the individual has to meet his or her karmic debt—usually under increasingly more dire conditions. Seen in this light, losing one's soul to sensational experiences in life, whether it be through alcohol, drugs, or indulgent sex of any kind, is akin to self-destruction.

Women today are also marching under a banner—the feminist movement. The most wonderful thing about a movement is that you can so easily forget who you really are. How easy it is to get lost under the guise of what is the accepted thinking at the moment. Nothing of any real consequence will ever be worked out on a collective basis. You can only work on your own individual self, when you realize the purpose of your own life.

Movements such as women's liberation are counterproductive to the soul's development. The approach—making waves in all the wrong directions—is mass-thinking and group karma in a most negative form. It is really a way of avoiding confrontation with the self. Your freedom or oppression is never dependent on someone else's authority.

Many women are beginning to think that their main role is in the business world—in competition with men—as if there were nothing pleasurable about being a woman, and all that being a woman implies. As a consequence of indoctrination, women are beginning to praise and value all the wrong things: competitiveness, militancy, sexual parity, and so forth. They're becoming more masculine, and in turn, men are becoming more feminine. The roles are blurring, and much is due to the fact that few people identify sufficiently with reincarnation and roles selected for spiritual growth.

A woman—because she has *selected* to be a woman—has assumed in the essence-state the responsibilities of womanhood. There are distinct differences between men and women. If you came into this incarnation as a woman, it is because you needed to experience and express the things that are truly the domain of women: intuitive feelings, refinement, gentleness, submissiveness, beauty, and motherhood. If you have a subsequent need to be aggressive, strong, and physical, you will have your chance when you choose to incarnate as a man!

Today's emphasis on abortion also needs to be examined, inasmuch as we disconnect ourselves from our responsibilities by not appreciating that life is a continual, reciprocal flow. With abortion we are actually cutting off the stream of life, not allowing its full expression. Again, we justify our attitudes with all sorts of rationalizations—overpopulation, famine, and economics.

Souls in the spirit-world must reincarnate, but in order to do so, they need the physical vehicle for expression on Earth. When an abortion takes place, the soul doesn't have a chance to come into this experience. Having prepared itself for a sojourn on this planet, its incarnation is halted. The source is cut off. For this reason more than anything else, abortion should be seriously reexamined. We must give life a way of expressing itself naturally, without our human minds maneuvering and interfering in God's domain.

In practicing birth control, not only are people taking in foreign matter, which is damaging, but again they're cutting off the channel for souls who have a need to experiment here on Earth, in this type of setting, under particular challenges. Just as we were given this opportunity, other souls are waiting in the wings. By employing birth control indiscriminately, as society encourages, we do not avail these souls the chance to enter this world and to interact with us. As a result, we cut off our own opportunities. Birth control, like anything else, comes right back to the discernment and choice of the individual. When a soul has a need to incarnate, its communication will be picked up intuitively and the desire for procreation will be overwhelming. This, too, is God's domain, and societal attitudes about overpopulation should not interfere with the process.

ROLE PLAYING

Whatever you do, if you don't do it with love, you have done absolutely nothing. And that love has to come from an inner awareness. Your capacity to love can diminish or increase: The more you express it, the more love you have to express. The less you use it, the faster you lose it! Love begets love.

There are a lot of serious people who truly want to work on themselves, and make tremendous efforts in that direction. But they undertake the task as a duty, a chore.

They want to work out karma but they approach it like homework, with an attitude of resentment, a chip on their shoulder, as if they were serving a jail sentence. They think that when they've done their time, they'll be free. As long as karma is considered a duty, and you have not brought your love and understanding to your challenges in life, you have not touched on your karmic debts. You are wasting your opportunities.

It can't be emphasized enough the importance of the love factor that must enter into everything that you do, every minute of the day. Your every breath must exude love—to God, to your fellow human beings, to yourself, to everything you encounter—whatever you're involved in. If love does not permeate your entire being, you are not accomplishing a blessed thing.

Many people play by the rules; they make all the righteous moves. But they leave out of their actions the most essential ingredient—love.

During meetings at the Gurdjieff Foundation, we would sit in meditation before beginning a session. There was a fellow there who always sat in the lotus position, a fixed grin covering his face. His mask never changed. Whether you talked or ignored him, his grin was perpetual. Perhaps he believed he could psych himself into bliss. I must confess I was often tempted to prick him with a pin just to see how he would react!

We all have the tendency to assume different roles at different times in our lives. The most painful kind of role playing must be *worrying about what other people think of you.* Trying to live up to others' expectations is selfish. It is merely approval-seeking and therefore false and egotistical. You want to fit into their mold, and therefore you consider everything you do—not for your sake, but for their sake. It becomes a charade: "If I don't do this to please them, they won't like me." You set out to maintain an image you think they have of you. You compromise yourself. You lead yourself into it, hating every moment of it, all to preserve the image you think they have of you! Role playing is an exercise in futility.

Recently a man came to see me for a reading. He was a very handsome, tall, dynamic individual in his forties. From the start, I felt uncomfortable about what was projected. I proceeded with great care. The very first spread of the cards gave me his general atmosphere. It quickly revealed a love/sex problem. I closed the deck and went into the second spread, but it did not say much. Throughout the reading the problem dominated.

It was indicated that in his career he rendered an enormous service to the public, although in direct conflict with his personal and emotional life. There was no romantic relationship indicated at all. Yet the need for such an exchange was overwhelming. It was a long session that touched deeply on his conflicting problem, a burden he had suffered throughout his life. The final outcome of the reading revealed that he would balance his life by giving up his profession to find the type of work akin to his nature. It was also projected that he would ultimately marry.

When it was over he asked me, "Do you know what I do?" I shook my head. Lowering his voice be said, "I'm a priest." Frankly, I was surprised. He looked more like a football player. Over coffee, he told me of the inner struggle he had been going through, torn between duty to church and his true emotions. His family had been very religious and had imposed the priesthood on him. He determined now that he would leave the church. His strong need for the expression of personal love and marriage, which he had deliberately denied himself, would now find fulfillment.

We often assume a role, which we act out as a form of duty, not as an expression of inner love. This man had the role of priest forced on him. Through not wanting to hurt his parents, he had forgone his own needs.

The reading merely confirmed his inner awareness that he could never resolve his life as long as this duality existed, no matter how good a job he did as a priest. By the time I saw him to the door, he was a changed person. New life shone upon his face. He had made a monumental decision.

There are other, more common roles thrust on us. Retirement is a favorite right now, and it is surely one of the worst concepts that has ever been introduced in our society. For most, it immediately proclaims, "Life is over, finished." Life is a field of experimentation at every age. Yet so many retire and no longer experiment with anything. Not only does dullness and lethargy set in, but all faculties, physical and mental, slowly deaden. For too many, mandatory retirement is a death sentence imposed by law.

There is another horrible phrase: "to settle down." Such sayings should be stricken from any language. We've all heard of or seen on television the Russian Georgians who live to such ripe old ages—sometimes reaching 160. Obviously their states of mind are entirely different from ours. They know nothing of retirement. They work hard for their daily bread, and they play with equal vigor. Moreover they do not equate with sickness. They are not what we would regard as a sophisticated, intellectual people, but they simply live life matter-of-factly—in elemental harmony—*enjoying* it to the full.

Their elderly are revered by the young, rather than looked down upon or discarded, as they are elsewhere. Life for them has an entirely different meaning. Fatherhood at age 100 is fairly common. The seventies and eighties are considered youthful. Climate, terrain, and diet are certainly contributing factors, but love is the foundation of their existence, as expressed through the family unit and the concern they have for each other. Singing and harmonizing with one another is an integral part of their lives; they are a people of great spirit, totally relaxed, and free of tension. Recently, one of the "older" women there was interviewed by a newspaper and asked to what she attributed her longevity. Her answers were simple: "I smoke three packs of cigarettes a day, and pipes in between, and I drink three glasses of vodka washed down with a bottle of wine." She never mentioned yogurt.

MY NEPHEW, AMNON

As a child I was very close to Joe, the younger of my two elder brothers. We confided in one another and had an unspoken bond of understanding between us. Joe moved to Israel as a young man and soon married a Sabra girl, Neima, and their love for one another and their children was beautiful. Their first child was a girl, whom they named Varda. A few years later, they had a son, Amnon.

When I first met my nephew, he was a little under two years of age. I had come to visit Joe and his family and stayed with them, sharing a room with little Amnon. He was an extraordinary child, with bright golden hair and whimsical eyes that knew only laughter. He brought joy wherever he went. Anyone who saw him was caught up in his sunny atmosphere.

They were a very musical family. Neima was a teacher of music, and Varda was studying piano. With music all around me, my own interest in piano was stimulated and I started working on a Beethoven sonata. I practiced daily for the pure enjoyment of it, and Amnon soon knew the piece as well as I did. Sitting nearby, he was able to hum the entire thing, from beginning to end, loving every minute of it and smiling at me. If I paused, he picked up where I left off and then I would join him and we would continue the movement together.

Often he woke up in the middle of the night humming Beethoven. I thought this was fantastic, but at 4:00 A.M. I really didn't appreciate it. He was a happy baby, and never fretted no matter where he was taken. So when he started a performance in the middle of the night, I would go over to his crib, apologize to him, and pick him up in my arms. He would smile and continue to hum as I carried him out into the moonlight and placed him in his playpen in the backyard, telling him I had to get some sleep. I could still hear him humming as I walked back into the house.

The next time I visited Israel, he was a man, celebrating his bar mitzvah at the age of thirteen. He had a bounce in his step, and his hair was still the color of the sun. We had long talks, he and I, and I marveled at his insights, his beautiful feelings of spirituality. I realized that whatever he chose to do with his life, he would be a great success. I also noticed how he and Varda had become as close as Joe and I had been. They shared every secret and knew what the other was thinking.

But on this visit, as on my previous one, I began to see first-hand how the people of Israel lived with the notion of war as a daily possibility. Military installations were everywhere; everyone served in the army in some capacity; and children were particularly influenced by all of this. I didn't like any of it, but my brother had become a devoted patriot. We often disagreed on this subject.

As Amnon went into high school, his education became directed toward the military. He developed a passion for tanks, guns, and artillery and wrote me letters describing his dreams of serving his country. My brother Joe became increasingly proud of his son's interests. The army wanted Amnon to be an officer, but he insisted on joining as a soldier. With his intelligence and enthusiasm, he did very well and was quickly promoted from one rank to the next.

I was very upset about all of this and wrote to Amnon and his father protesting that no one in our family had ever served in the military before. I urged Amnon to think in terms of life as constructive, as something to be preserved for creative purposes, but it was all too clear that the army had become his whole life. Israel was unique, my brother insisted in his letters. Survival left no choice and to serve in the army there was an honorable duty. But inside I knew he and his wife were deeply concerned and worried.

Then, in October of 1973, on Yom Kippur came the surprise attack. I immediately thought of Amnon, realizing the tanks would be the first to go into battle, but I couldn't get through for several days as the lines were jammed with high-priority calls. Joe phoned me, at last, to tell me that Amnon had been wounded. I had a sinking feeling in my solar plexus and tried to get details out of him, but the connection was terrible and the conversation ended abruptly.

The next day I called and learned that Amnon was about to be operated on. I was relieved in some way to know that he was no longer at the front lines, but the strange foreboding wouldn't go away.

Two days later, at the age of nineteen, Amnon died. It was one of the most painful things I have ever experienced. I loved him so deeply. I couldn't see why this wonderful boy, who had brought so much happiness to everyone who knew him, should have had his life cut so short. Day after day, with tears in my eyes, I asked *"Why?"* I began to question everything I believed about life, because something so dreadful had happened to someone I loved so dearly. Caught up in this tragedy, my connection with my beliefs was temporarily severed. Amnon's family was numb with grief. His sister, Varda, was inconsolable.

Later when I learned the details of what had happened, I saw how the pieces of the puzzle began to fit in terms of reincarnation. Amnon had been a tank commander, with a crew of three men. In the midst of battle, deep in the Sinai Desert, their turret gun malfunctioned. It was Amnon's duty to climb out of the tank and determine what was wrong. While outside, he was hit by shrapnel and thrown to the ground, unable to move. He shouted at his men to proceed, that his life was over, but they refused to obey him and managed to get him back behind the lines to a field hospital. The doctors discovered he was paralyzed from the waist down. They were hopeful, but Amnon was convinced he wouldn't recover and became withdrawn. Right up to the end he refused to see anyone, not even his fiancee, or his family. His men were supposed to return to the front as soon as the tank was repaired. At the last minute they were relieved of their duties and a new crew was assigned to the tank, which was subsequently destroyed, killing all four men inside.

It was obvious that the first three men who had been with Amnon were meant to live, and it would seem that Amnon had programmed himself for but a twenty-year span in this lifetime. He had entered into the war with great zeal, which most Israelis have when defending their homeland. It would be difficult not to be caught up in this fever. Defense of one's country has become a blinding concern. Universally it is believed that fighting is an only means of survival. Will we ever learn that war never was, never will be the answer? Patriotism is nothing but mass hysteria and even under extreme pressure we as individuals must extricate ourselves from marching under such false banners. For the entire Middle East, the conflicts are clearly the result of group karma. The karmic debt will only be erased when individuals on both sides of the conflict learn to love and live with each other.

Only when we as individual human beings recognize but one banner—*that life is sacred*—all weapons will fall away from us, and war will be no more.

Each person meets with his or her own personal karma first even where groups are involved. In Amnon's case, as I came to understand it, his life was irrevocably tied to an important karmic debt. He was not vindictive or possessed by hatred of the Arabs, yet he was drawn strongly into the military. It was apparent in terms of reincarnation that he had chosen a life that was to end in his own sacrifice.

After a period of mourning, I sat down to a séance cer-

tain that Amnon would come through, and he did. His communication was brief and to the point. "Nobody knows it,"
he said, "but I suffered four wounds. I was hit by a 135." He
explained that a 135 was a Russian gun. Then he urged me to
deliver an important message to my brother, Joe: "Tell my
father that I am alive. Tell him to stop mourning."

My brother had indeed plunged into an all-consuming
grief, and I immediately wrote to him reporting what
Amnon had said. The day after the séance I had met a man
who was an authority on the wars of the Middle East, and I
asked him about the 135. He told me it was a Russian anti-
personnel weapon. I included this information in my letter
in the hope that Joe would believe me. "You know I know
nothing about guns," I said. "So where did it come from?
Obviously, something exists on a higher plane and comes
through when the source is tapped and the channel is open.

"Perhaps so," he replied by return post. "I wish I could
believe what you've told me. I wish I could believe that
Amnon is still alive somewhere."

There is no greater tragedy in human experience than to
lose a loved one, especially for a parent to lose a child. And
yet here, too, we must remove our finite thinking and conceptualize life as an eternal continuum, whereby the soul
sheds the body and metamorphosizes in a different form in a
different dimension. Death is never final because with each
death there is a new beginning.

God bless you, Amnon.

MOVING ON

After our trip to Badgastein, my father felt we should
visit Germany, since it was so close. I was born in what is
now East Berlin, and I thought it would be interesting to go
back and see our neighbors, the place we lived, and the
school I attended. So we arranged to spend three days in Berlin.

I had never really wanted to return before, because of the

atrocities and the horrors of the war. I really didn't want to stir those memories. But on our way there, I began to get excited. The idea of revisiting the places of my childhood appealed to my imagination. I was in for quite a shock.

I had been only eight when we left East Berlin, but the streets were still familiar, so much so that I could take my father by the hand and lead the way. As we arrived at our street, Chorinerstrasse, I was startled to see that the house we had lived in was no longer there. We learned it had been bombed and rebuilt. It was beyond recognition. I then looked for my school. Instead, I found an empty lot. It had been bombed to rubble as well. *All the places that I remembered from my childhood no longer existed.*

That told me a lot. The beginning of my life was over and done with. There was no going back, no need to review it anymore. The karmic experience of that past was finished. I no longer depended on those memories. What had taken place in my childhood in Germany were merely experiences along the path of many experiences yet to come. It was obvious I should leave it alone, be done with it, without sentiment, and move on.

A similar thing happened only recently. I discovered the building where I was married no longer existed. It was bulldozed and a parking lot was put in its place. That part of my life too was no more. When the physical places of your past are gone, you have no choice but to view it correctly. The past is dead and buried. There is but one urgent message here: You must move on.

Our understanding is always enlarged as we reflect on the experiences that transpired before. We can evaluate and see things for what they really were: what we utilized, how we could have done better, and so forth. And if we could see all our past lives, and all that we have either built or destroyed, we could immediately make tremendous strides in this lifetime. Once this connection is made, we realize that being here this time around is not an accident or an isolated experience. We then have a fantastic overview of what our deeds must be and the urgency and overwhelming importance of our purpose is made clear. Thus, we move forward.

When you really understand the workings of karma, and recognize that what you are today is a result of what you were in previous lives, and the integral part that you have played in your destiny, then you are ready to free yourself of karmic debts. This potential is available to us all the time. We can work out our karma in one lifetime, living in such a conscious, loving way that longevity without limitation could be ours.

Such consciousness would take the height of awareness (and even that height is unlimited). To be so totally conscious, so totally and deliberately directive in every moment of your being, every second of every day—in your living, in your action, in your exchanges, in your humility, in your whole being—this is the road to freedom, perfection, and everlasting life.

Chapter Eleven

What Are You Going to Do About It Now?

The spiritual mind is open, receptive and loving,
recognizing change as the only constant.

I KNEW A MAN who used to say, "I'm an atheist," and I would always quickly add, "Thank God!" He felt my way of thinking was *interesting*, but certainly not practical. A lot of people will say to me, if they don't accept the concepts yet want to be kind, "You're way out—but you're interesting. I've never met anyone like you before." And that is what I'm sure of: Anyone who meets me—or you for that matter—has never met anyone like us before. We're *all* unique.

People are generally so involved with themselves, so automatic, they rarely lift an eyebrow. Sometimes I like to talk about my beliefs just to see the reaction. When you throw a new thought at most people, a thought which is a little different from the habitual fare, they must stop and think— they can't help themselves. "Where did that come from? I haven't heard that before," they say.

Look how God expresses through people, through the animal kingdom, through nature, and through everything. We live in such a fantastic, multifaceted universe. Why do we limit ourselves to habit, dogma, ritual, narrow-mindedness? We too are multifaceted because we, too, are the representatives of God. We are part of the magnificent imagination of the higher intelligence, the result of God's contemplation. We are the expression of God. And if we do not live life by this ideal, then the limitations we experience are of our own making.

Who and what we meet is who and what we are. When we judge others we judge ourselves. The drunk you see on the street is you! And you are him! Your recognition and judgment of another is a mirror of yourself, at one time or another, either as a possibility, or having been there already. Therefore, you *know*.

We are enormously rich beings, with unlimited inner resources. We truly do not know, and as yet have not realized what wonderful capacities lie dormant within us. But on a subconscious level we *do* know it, and it is that subconscious memory that we want to stir and awaken to bring our lives into fuller, more purposeful, expression. When you live life from moment to moment, from breath to breath, and your totality is present every second, then there is nothing left but to be grateful and give thanks. Everything you encounter in that spirit is wonderful. It's the best thing that could happen to you. You must give thanks no matter how painful the experience. When you really understand the benefits and the challenges constantly staring you in the face, and you apply your higher self in a practical way, you glimpse something new in yourself. A memory of the past embedded in your subconscious being has been tapped and utilized. A new channel is now wide open.

This channel brings you in touch with yourself on a deeper level. It beckons and urges you to express love—to yourself, to others, and to all of creation. Everything that happens in your experience that is seemingly bad is simply because you have not expressed love at one time or another.

It may not come back directly from the person you have slighted, but it will come back to you, nevertheless—maybe years later, maybe even in another lifetime, or possibly in the very next moment. Time is never a factor.

Every difficult experience in your life can either be met positively or negatively. If the response is negative, the results will be negative, telling you over and over again, "You have not expressed love."

The power is within. You can erase everything, you can clean the slate any moment you decide. You can start anew—eliminating karma accumulated from past lives—the moment you begin to love. When love determines your every moment of living, karma is canceled, making it nonexistent. Letting go of the past is the only road to freedom, your true liberation.

We have a tremendous need to express love, and this is our greatest conflict. We seem to be able to deal with anything but love. And yet this is all we are—love. Love is God. God is Love. It doesn't matter what words are used—God, cosmic consciousness, higher intelligence, universal awareness—they're all the same. Thank God, God is not dependent on man-made, spiritually diluted religions, cults, or labels.

Everything talks to us. No one can escape his or her own person. Sooner or later, we have to confront ourselves. Once we wake up to the truth, once we know it, we can no longer run away from ourselves and our surroundings, from everything that is life. We set in motion new dynamics, creating a new world for ourselves and others. Life becomes holy, sacred, something to be revered. With such feelings of reverence toward everything and everyone, you will discover a different quality in your encounters with the world. Openness, enthusiasm, wonder, fearlessness—the byproducts of love. Love opens up all the inspiring resources within you; indeed, it unlocks all the secrets of the universe.

Nothing need be strange to us. Nothing is foreign. The subconscious mind knows all. Truly, there is nothing new under the sun. When life gets complicated, sophisticated, involved, or troubled, it is because our own distorted thinking has obscured our memory of the truth. We need to awaken our memory. We need to stir it to such a degree that we can express life with greater profundity and purpose. Above all, we need to keep life simple. We can only do this by tapping the force of love. Once you embody the inner feeling of love, you see the whole world differently, and a new vision is yours.

There is far more beauty in people than we wish to see. Look for that beauty in others. It's not that hidden. Too often we look only for the ugliness but does finding it make us more beautiful? Why focus on flaws, blemishes, or things you can criticize? Can they make you more important? Is this the power you seek? Turn your energy around. Look for the good. Then mentally and imaginatively imbue other persons with it; then give them the end result of the good you see in them.

A seeming miracle will result, for unbeknownst to them, *that which you visualize in other persons as good, they will vie to produce!* They will magically respond. Just as disorder or critical judgment of other persons can be picked up mentally, without them knowing it, the recipients will endeavor to live up to your high (or low) opinion of them. All criticism—even so-called constructive criticism—has its roots in hate. For we must hate, if only a little, to sit in judgment of another. There is a mental interaction which takes place on the subconscious level between all living beings without the utterance of a single word. Most people are unaware of why they respond positively or negatively to you. Instinctively, they react to your view of them.

We need to acquire, learn, and exercise humility and gratitude toward everyone and everything. We need constant reminders that we have not created ourselves in the primal sense. The true source of creation—whatever your concept of that may be—must be acknowledged and recognized. We are not here to compete with our Creator. We are here to align our energies and join forces with God, and in so doing to become the powerhouses we are meant to be. Every minute of the day we ought to give thanks for the opportunity to be alive. The most precious gift of life is to be treasured.

When sitting in meditation or self-contemplation, start by giving thanks to God. Build on that. This is the constructive premise to unfold and rediscover the self. We really don't discover anything, truly we're not creators. We are only re-creators. Any masterpiece you can think of isn't creation—it's *re*-creation. God creates, the artist re-creates. Creation is fulfilled already. We don't create anything new. But the importance here is that in re-creating, we rediscover ourselves and our connection with the Oneness. Our function begins with "re-" . . . We need to reconfirm the truth about ourselves, and our relationship to everything else in the universe. Above all, we need to know our place and return to the Godhead. To know is to use and apply our wisdom and love, to use our higher intelligence.

Likewise, we really don't own anything at all: Nothing is ours. But everything is ours to *use*. Knowing this can make quite a difference. Nothing belongs to us, is owned by us—not the mind, ideas, health, the air we breathe, and certainly not anything material. But we can use everything. Everyone can. In one sense, nothing belongs to us. Yet, in the truer sense, everything is ours if used properly. By acting in accordance with our true needs, we would become less possessive of people, property, and the material things of life. We may take something, and utilize it, then put it aside for others to use, and whenever that need is there again, it will always be available. That is the true wealth of life.

If only we would regard all our experiences as wonderful and necessary, we could recognize the essential process of learning. If we would but see life from a larger perspective, and realize why this sojourn on Earth is so all-important in our development, then instantly our attitude would change, particularly in handling the more difficult experiences we encounter in life. Rather than allowing our problems to engulf us, we would welcome them and work toward their proper resolution. This is the key to self-awareness that opens the gates of enlightenment. All problems challenge you: Welcome them as your greatest opportunity.

You can only know the truth through your own experiences. A truth is not a truth until *you* experiment with it and find it to be a truth for yourself. If you were given the greatest truth in the universe on a silver platter, it would be meaningless unless you had tested and verified it for yourself. Then the truth must be declared, confirmed, and reaffirmed in and through us, but this can only be accomplished with an open mind and determined application. How else can you demonstrate a truth but by experimentation? We must apply what we know and make it tangible. This process helps us make discoveries and to learn more about ourselves so we can move on. The truth is always creative, useful, and positive. Truth is the foundation on which we must build our lives.

One of the things that happens when we begin to change and make new discoveries while working on ourselves is that we immediately want to convince and convert everyone else to our newfound ways. The purpose of self-discovery is not to shove it down everybody else's throat. Let people be. Allow others to make their own discoveries. Once we've made the slightest change and latched on to a new wavelength, we tend to assume the role of a know-it-all.

This self-proclaimed expert role is assimilated all too quickly, creating a negative atmosphere, regardless of whether our ideas are sound or not. For example, a sick person isn't literally saying to himself, "I want to be sick." Such individuals may not be aware of what attracts sickness into their lives. If you were to come along and say to them, "You asked for it. You attracted and created it for yourself," no matter how true, at once you have cut off all communication with them.

You don't have to explain yourself to others. You do have to explain yourself to yourself. *Your own business is a full-time job.* No matter what the truth may be, or how much you may want to share it, no matter how good your intentions, if you do not inspire others by loving example, you have missed your communication with them.

It cannot be said often enough: Don't proselytize. You don't need to convince others; you need to convince yourself. When you are truly convinced of something, you no longer need to sway other people to your way of thinking. You can leave them alone. It's only while struggling with yourself that you have the need to impose your ideas on others. When you actually *become* what you have learned, your message comes across naturally; it attracts unto itself. "When the pupil is ready, the teacher appears." It really does not matter who the teacher or the pupil is—they're one and the same.

A young man in his early twenties came to me for a reading. He told me he was studying meditation and that he hoped to teach it someday. As we went into the reading, he began to bristle. He controlled his anger for a while, but finally burst forth. "I resent all this—that you are such an authority," he exclaimed.

He asked me why I laughed at his remark, probably thinking I should have been insulted, and I said, "It's uncanny. I'm not your authority at all, but look at your preconceived ideas that have made me your authority. That is what you resent." He listened, but it hurt because I had thrown it right back at him. Throughout the reading he interrupted time and again. "What does that mean?" or "Well, that could apply to anyone," when in fact they were specific things pertaining to him. He shunned his own responsibility, made me his authority, and then resented me for it. He left with the same chip on his shoulder that he had walked in with. He never got the point that he was his own authority.

And that is the very point of this book. The only authority is you, through your testing of the material herein. Unless you try it out, play with it, apply it in your daily life, you will never know who the real authority is. Make no one an authority who is quick to give out the rules of life. Life is something you must be open-minded about, allowing for all possibilities. There is only one truth but many ways to arrive at it. Travel your own road. Subject everything to your own interpretation. When you take command of your own life, you will never allow anybody else to navigate for you. There is nothing anyone can say that you don't already know. As has been said before, "The book you read is the book you write."

With all my heart, what I hope comes across with utmost clarity is the fact that *you don't have to stay stuck.* You can move on, whatever your circumstance, to a better place by unsticking yourself the moment you decide. Often, during a reading something comes up that is painful. People feel they must elaborate, explain it away, so I let them talk. Most people are living somewhere in the past or in the future, and their future is always a projection of their past experience. The present is completely absent and yet these are the very people who will talk to you about "reality." Only their problems are real. I've learned it's important to let them go over their hurts and traumas. On and on, the details, the justifications that come from everywhere to substantiate their stuckness. When at last they're through and exhausted from their tale of woe, having lived it over a million times, the inevitable question comes up. "Tell me, what are you going to do about it *now*?" Often they look at me as if I haven't been listening or were unsympathetic. Neither is the case.

We are today people in a today world. We cannot undo the deeds of the past. We cannot alter the facts of yesterday. Indeed, yesterday is dead and gone. But we can shape our tomorrows by the way we live today. What you do *now* is everything, and everything is forever talking to you.